SHIPPING CONTAINER HOMES

HOMES

A GUIDE ON HOW TO BUILD AND MOVE INTO SHIPPING CONTAINER HOMES WITH EXAMPLES OF PLANS AND DESIGNS

Contents

An Introduction to Shipping Container Homes

History

The shipping container was created in the 1950s by Malcolm McLean. Since then, it has revolutionized the transport industry, offering efficient, convenient, and structurally sound containers to deliver goods in bulk. Shipping containers are sturdy, corrugated steel boxes that can be delivered full of goods. Today, they can be found in surplus all over the world.

It took another three decades for the first patent to be filed for the repurposing of the shipping container into habitable buildings. The idea was novel and the implications massive. These strong, readily available containers could be cheaply and quickly transformed into homes, schools, shops, even apartment complexes or sports halls.

Over the last few decades, the use of shipping container homes for commercial and residential structures has become mainstream in Europe. They provide emergency shelters, housing for heavily populated cities, shopping centers, schools, and a host of other needed structures. Shipping containers lend themselves to these purposes because they can be modified in any way imaginable. They can be modified to suit the needs of any given structure.

The use of shipping containers for habitable structures has not been confined to Europe. All over the world, these readily available materials have offered sustainable and affordable architecture for those that need it. Given the growing need for green, cheap, and sustainable building solutions, shipping container architecture has become a growing global phenomenon. Now, unique and beautiful homes can be built by anyone, customized exactly to their preferences, and created with a fraction of time and expense required by traditional homes.

Benefits

There are a huge number of benefits to building and living in shipping container homes. As mentioned above, they are structurally strong, affordable, and sustainable. They can be extremely energy efficient, and there are more than 50 million surplus shipping containers in the U.S. alone. With so many in the current economic climate who struggle to find affordable homes, these sturdy, valuable structures can provide an easy alternative to traditional homes.

Here are just a few of the benefits of shipping container homes:

Quick to build – Instead of the months required to build traditional homes, shipping container homes can be built in a matter of days.

Environmentally friendly – Rather than building the shell of your home from bricks, cement, or wood, shipping containers offer a readymade shell with low environmental impact. Even the use of the shipping container itself is economical, as it is the reuse of materials which would otherwise go to waste.

Extremely strong – Anyone who has seen shipping containers firsthand knows just how strong they are. They are made from steel that can easily endure harsh environments. In fact, shipping containers have been used as emergency shelters during hurricanes and during wartime.

Affordable – This is a huge consideration. Traditional homes can cost hundreds of thousands of dollars, while it is possible to make a shipping container home for as low as $14,000. This will vary with the modifications, number of shipping containers used, and whether it is DIY or built with the help of a contractor, but it is possible to build and move into your home with only minimal expenses.

Capable of transport – Though it is not simple to transport a shipping container home after it has been placed upon the foundation, it is possible and has been done countless times. This is something that simply cannot be done with traditional homes.

Like anything, it helps to do your homework before getting started. Over the course of this book, we'll be exploring all you need to know to obtain, modify, place, finish, and move into your shipping container home. We'll be going through each detail and offering tips that will help you to avoid any delays or costly mistakes.

Throughout the following chapters, you will be shown a real-life shipping container home in the process of being built, from the plans to the final product. The picture to the left is the finished product, a beautiful and elegant home crafted for under $20,000, and sturdy enough to last several lifetimes with minimal repairs or expenses.

And this is just one way that your shipping container home can be customized and created. Your home can be easily and quickly crafted to fill your every need

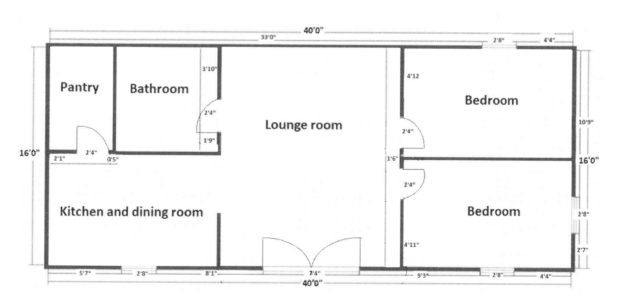

Floor Plan

So, whether you want to create your home with a minimal of costs, use environmentally-friendly and sustainable architecture in the creation of your home, or have a home created to your exact specifications, the shipping container home is perfect to meet your needs. In a time where the world is eagerly seeking green alternatives to traditional homes, the shipping container home offers a simple and effective solution.

The purpose of this guide is to provide a detailed walk-through of each step of the process of shipping container selection, transport, foundation, utilities, modification, and finishing. In each chapter, one aspect of construction is explored in depth, beginning with the planning process and extending through to the completed home. Included in each chapter are pictures of each stage of construction, providing real-life examples to help put the theory into tangible terms.

Chapter 1 – A Short Summary of the Process of Building and Moving into a Shipping Container Home

The shipping container home is easier to build and move into from start to finish than any traditional home. Many of the considerations are the same, but you will be working with a pre-established structural shell. The home can go up in a matter of weeks rather than months or years. This is the home of the future, and getting a jump on the opportunity now can save years of effort and thousands of dollars.

The first step is to plan your shipping container home. Explore your needs: the bedrooms, bathrooms, and utilities you will need in your home. Then explore the budget that all of these carefully considered needs will require. Plan the budget well, considering additional expenses and taking zoning laws into account in the building design.

Next, you will need to locate both your building site and your containers. Consider new or used; assess the relevant issues of your building site. Consider whether the containers should be converted prior to shipping, onsite, or in an offsite workshop. Plan accordingly, ensuring that transportation is arranged both to ship the containers from the manufacturer to a nearby port and to transport the containers to the building site. Also plan to timetable so that services are established when necessary to power any tools needed onsite.

Prepare the site and foundation, ensuring that the soil can handle the load of the shipping container home, selecting the foundation that best suits your soil and building specifications. Place the home securely upon the foundations and secure the containers, attaching them to one another and to the foundations.

If the containers are being converted onsite, now is the time. Converting the containers involves cutting out sections of the steel walls of the containers to make space for doors, windows, and adjoining rooms. These openings will need to be fitted with frames and then doors and windows can be hung within them.

The next step is to build a roof, if you choose to do so. The flooring can then be addressed, whether you choose to cover the original flooring or remove and replace it. Next, the interior of the container is framed with stud walls. First fix services are then run, providing your container with initial plumbing, electrics, and telephone. During this process you will also see to the insulation of your container.

At this point, the home is nearly finished. Only a few steps remain. Install second fix services—running water, electric, sewage, and telephone lines—to their desired final location within the container. Finish the interior walls and flooring, and then clad the exterior of the container. Your home is then ready to be filled with furniture and occupied.

This is the entire process you need to follow to make sure that the home is completed. It's not an instant process, but it's well worth it, and you will love the process of custom building your home to your own specifications.

Chapter 2 – Planning

In order to know how you'd like to build your shipping container home, the first step is to plan it out. This means asking a few questions, exploring some of the practical needs and considerations before entering into the design phase. To get you started with this, here are some of the most important things to take into consideration:

What are your needs?

Consider how many bedrooms you want, how much floor space you and your family will require.

Consider the number of bathrooms and the extent of storage space necessary.

With a shipping container home, space is at a premium, so you'll want to consider how you can accommodate all of your needs as efficiently as possible.

Where will the home be built?

This question influences a number of other considerations, including zoning requirements for your intended location, soil type and foundation, and utilities planning.

The sections that follow explore many relevant considerations with respect to building location.

What's your budget?

This is another key consideration, as it will determine how many containers you can use, whether or not you will be able to hire contractors to help with the work, whether you intend to buy new, used, or one-time use containers, and a number of other factors.

The following section on financial planning explores many details of budgeting and offers an example of budgeting with a real-life shipping container home.

When would you like to have your home completed?

Timing is crucial when considering container delivery, equipment rental, and contracting arrangements.

Remember that in most instances, shipping container homes can be built in a matter of days or at most weeks.

Can you pull it off?

Do you have access to the skills, materials, financial resources, planning permission, and other necessities required for construction?

Financial planning

What can you afford? In most instances, this will determine your budget. Key considerations will include the cost of the land, the container, and the roof. Other important considerations are whether you have the skills, time, and resources to do the modification yourself, if you would like to hire contractors for the work, or if you intend to purchase the container pre-modified as a home.

The following chapters highlight a number of design choices and other factors which have a decisive impact upon the budget. Among these factors are whether you choose to purchase a new, used, or one-time use container, whether to include a roof, and the degree of modification you would like done to the container. Other important factors to consider are the required foundation type, utilities, and the transport and placement of the container.

Here is the budget used for the real-life example depicted above. This will give you a better idea of some of the possible costs.

Component	Quantity	Expenditure
Land (including taxes and fees)	1	$8000
Fees to professionals		$6500
Standard 40 Foot Container (Used in US)	2	$6300
Bathroom		$2500
Door (for both inside and outside)	5	$700
Kitchen		$3000
Insulation	1	$1800
Furniture		$3800
Windows	4	$850
Utilities		$3500
Internal fixes and fittings		$1500
Transport		$500
Flooring		$2300
Roof		$5500
Paint		$700
Walls inside home		$300
Unexpected costs	12%	$5730
Summary		$53480

One thing to remember regarding the example above is that the furnishings, flooring, and interior design have been chosen with luxury rather than economy in mind. Note that a 10% contingency cost has been added. Most construction endeavors, regardless of how well planned, include some unexpected expenses, so it's helpful to make sure you're prepared for such things when they occur.

Permits and Zoning Laws

Each country and, in most cases, each zoning district within a country has its own zoning regulations. These regulations determine which types of buildings can be placed on a given lot, as well as the density, height, and other requirements for structures within the zone. These regulations are complex, and it is not possible to provide all the details for every zone. However, here are a few details that will give some direction in becoming knowledgeable about your country's guidelines. Also included is a list of documents which are likely to be required by any country when designing your home.

Australia

Prior to major building work in Australia, you must obtain a permit from the local council. Check into your state's policy planning framework online, and then approach the council to find out the requirements for your state and for the council which governs your intended building site. They will be able to provide you a list of any documents required for your area or any regulations which should be considered during the design and planning phases.

New Zealand

New Zealand is a bit ahead of the game when it comes to shipping container homes. The Building Act of 2004 offers clear guidance for the construction of these homes. In most cases, they will require building consent, though if they are intended only for storage, then they may be exempt from this requirement. In addition, the territorial authority may choose to exempt your shipping container home from building consent, so long as it still meets the building codes. As in the examples above, the first step is to confer with the territorial authority to look into the specifics of your intended site and design.

United Kingdom

Any construction in the UK will require permission from the local council. The local planning authorities will each have their own specific regulations, so it is necessary to contact them before design and planning. The list of documents provided below will give you a head start, and they will be able to inform you if anything further is required.

United States

For most places in the U.S., construction requires a building permit. In order to obtain a building permit, first contact the local public works department. They will be able to inform you of the zoning status and requirements of your zone. With this information in hand, you can tailor your design to the regulations required.

If your building site is outside the city's zoning code, then it may not require a building permit. If you seek to build without a permit, then deliberately selecting a site outside of the zoning code is one way to avoid a bit of red tape. However, it should be remembered that these sites will have less access to power, water, and telephone lines, and will thus present other challenges.

General List of Documents Required

Though each council or local authority will have their own specifications and regulations, here are a few things you can expect to need. Remember that regulations may influence aspects of design, so it still helps to approach your local authority before spending valuable time and energy finalizing your design.

- Structural engineering plans and approval
- Site plan
- Building regulation drawings (to scale)
- Before and after elevations
- Fully dimensioned working drawings

Designing Your Home

So, once you've taken your needs into consideration and done your homework with regard to the local regulations, it's time to begin designing your home. Here is where you can get really creative. The simplest deign would be a single container home, and the sky's the limit on how far you can go with it. Two-story? Three? The possibilities are endless and they can be customized to fit your needs, whatever they might be.

It's most common to stick with single-story homes and to place containers next to one another until you reach your desired size. Connecting walls can be removed to increase the floor space of a room, and interior walls can be added to partition a container into multiple rooms. The basics are the bedroom, living room, kitchen, bathroom, and pantry, and all of these can be fit within a single 20-ft container if you're comfortable with a cozy living space.

A quick search online will offer many free software downloads that will help you to design your shipping container home. If you're uncomfortable doing this yourself, then you may want to factor the price of an architect into the budget. Usually, the quotes for such a small living space won't be unreasonable. However, give it a try and see how it works for you. You may be surprised how easy it is to design your home, and being in the driver's seat of the design process can be really fun.

Here are a number of sample plans which offer a wide range of different designs.

Sample Plans

These are just a few of the designs we could show you to showcase the potential for customization in shipping container homes. Have a look and let inspiration strike!

Plan 1

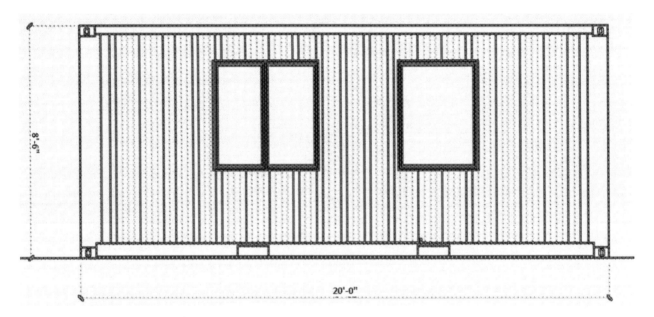

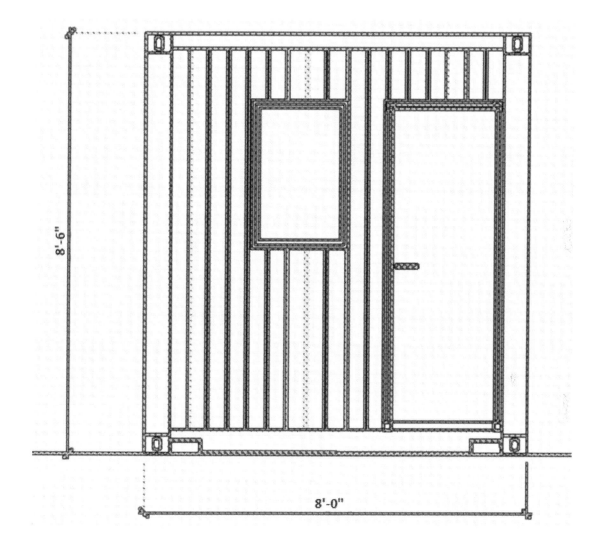

8'-6"

8'-0"

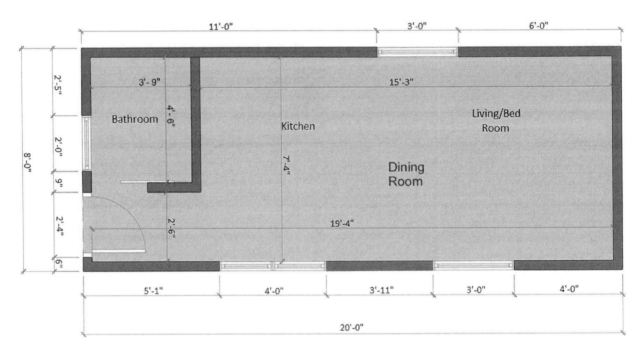

Plan 1 is ideal for a small, one-person dwelling. It offers 139 sq. ft. and is designed from a single 20-ft container and features a combination kitchen, dining room, living room, and bedroom. The ultimate in space efficiency and tiny living space.

Plan 2

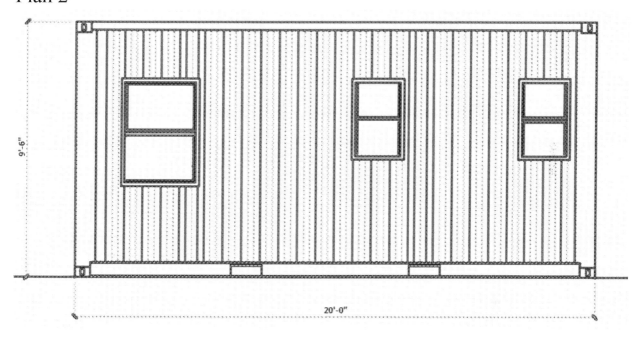

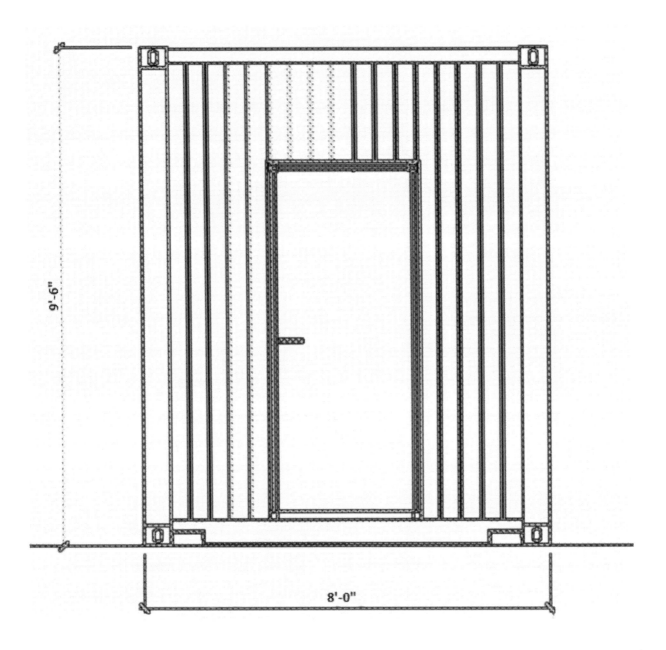

9'-6"

8'-0"

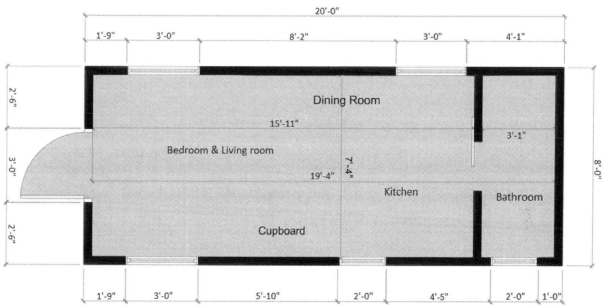

Plan 2 is another example of a single 20-ft container dwelling. It has been customized to offer a spacious bathroom and kitchen. The living room doubles as a bedroom and features two pull-out double beds, offering comfort whether sleeping or sitting. This economical design can comfortably house two people within 138 sq. ft.

Plan 3

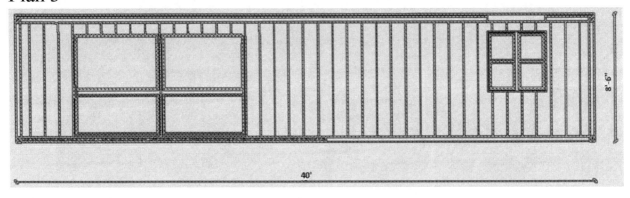

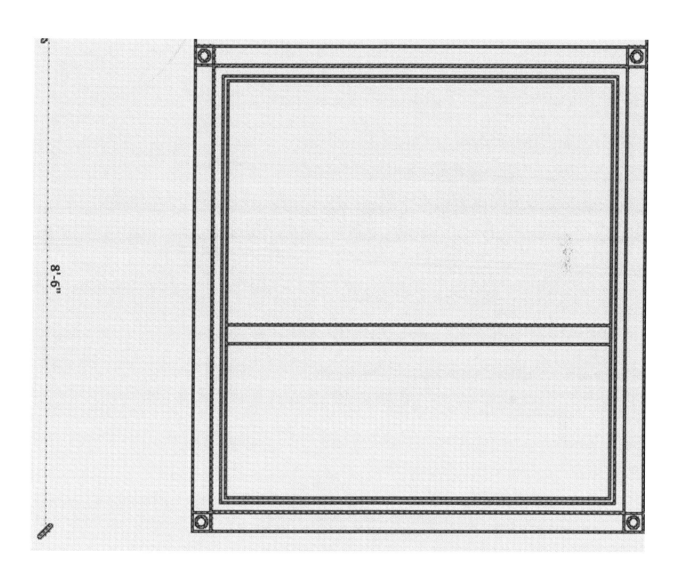

8'-6"

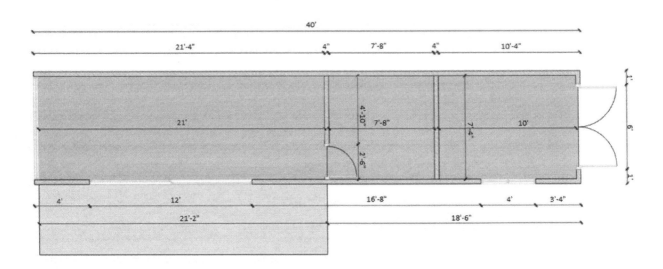

Plan 3 is designed from a single 40-ft. container and boasts a spacious open-plan living room which would be ideal for a sofa-bed. It features sliding glass doors which lead to an open deck. Also included is a second room ideal either for storage space or for a second bedroom.

Plan 4

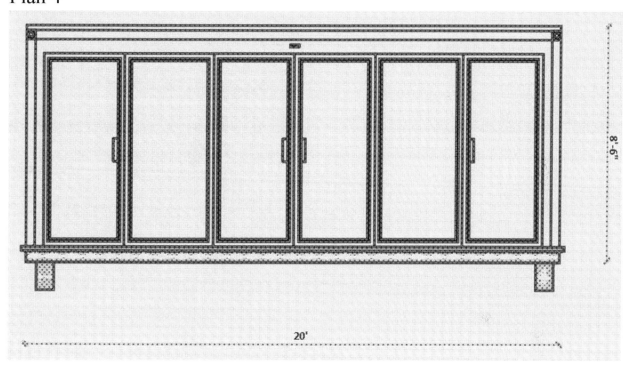

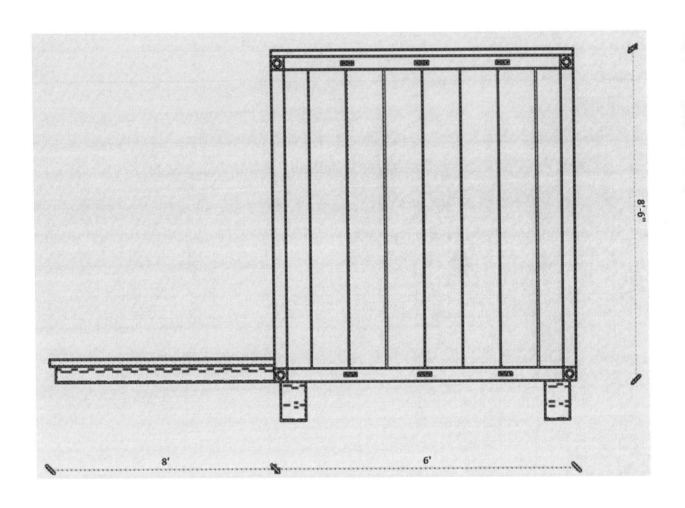

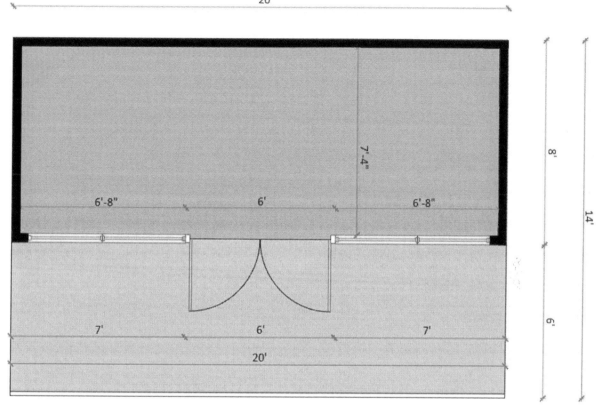

Plan 4 has been designed as a hunting lodge from a single 20-ft. container. It features a large open-plan living room with a small kitchen and bedroom off to the side. A full-length deck lines the front of the house, making it ideal for relaxing comfortably and taking in the night air. This offers a luxurious space for a single-person dwelling and can offer a comfortable space for two if a sofa bed is placed in the living room.

Plan 5

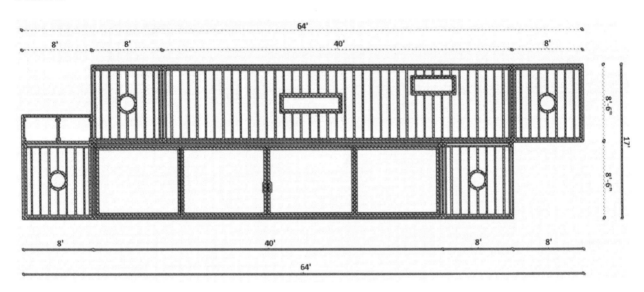

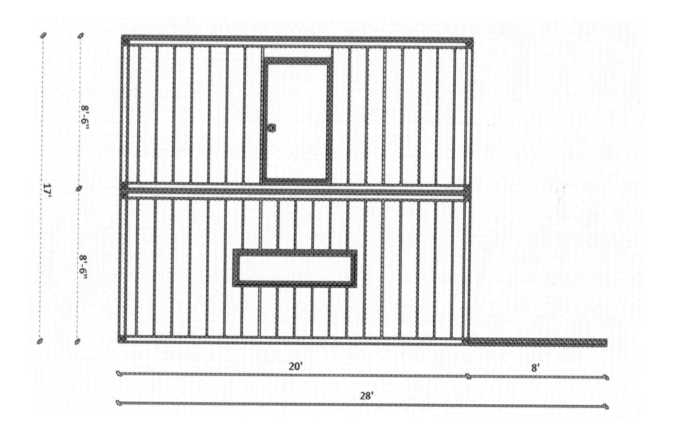

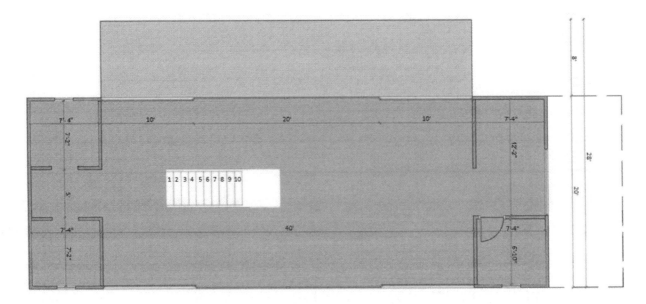

Upstairs:

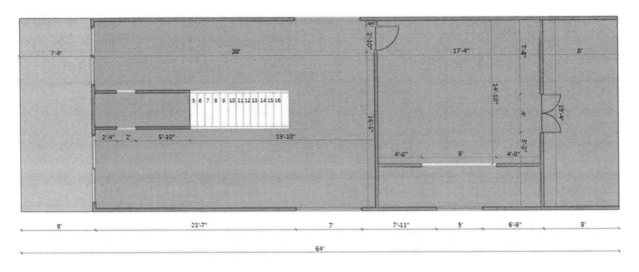

Plan 5 has been designed from four 40-ft. containers and four 20-ft. containers. It demonstrates the luxury possible with shipping container homes. This mansion features two floors, three bedrooms, three bathrooms, and an open-plan living room on both floors. Sliding glass doors on both the front and rear entrance, and a second-floor deck make this design an equal to any traditional home built with the height of decadence.

Plan 6

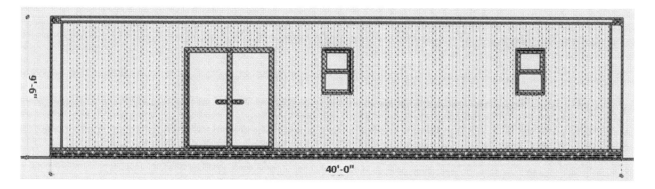

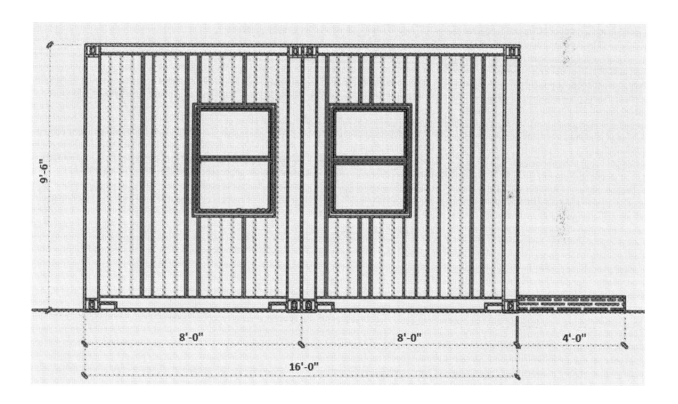

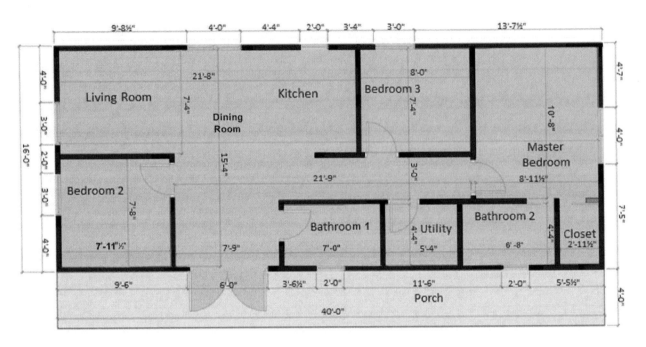

Plan 6 features three bedrooms and two bathrooms as well as a living room, dining room, kitchen, utility room, and closet. Ample living and storage space, all within two 40-ft. containers. In addition, there is a full-length deck lining the front of the dwelling. With 606 sq. ft., this dwelling can comfortably house three adults or a family of four.

Plan 7

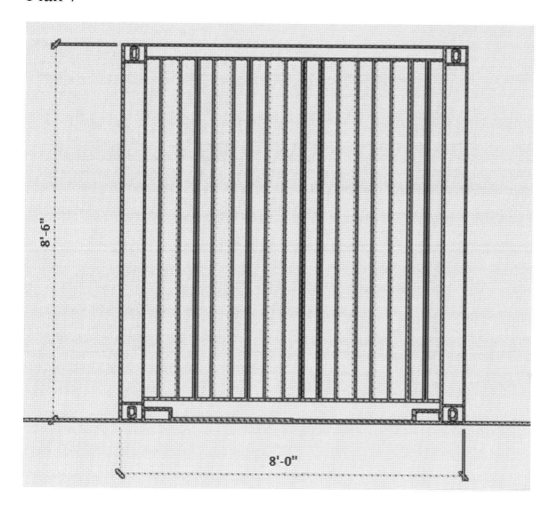

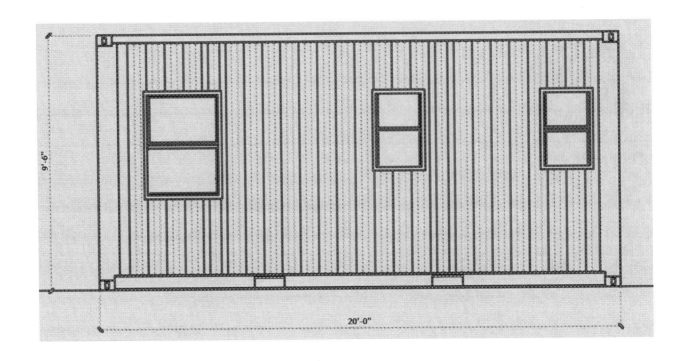

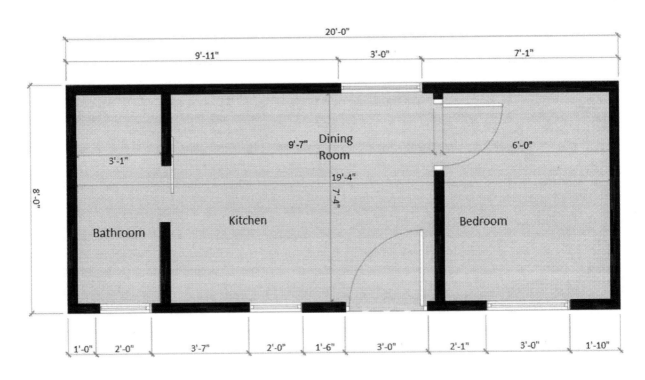

Plan 7 shows another design for a single 20-ft. container. This design combines spaciousness with efficiency, featuring a luxurious bathroom and master bedroom with a combined kitchen and dining room. This design is perfect for a single person or a couple, offering all the amenities necessary for a wilderness love nest within 135 sq. ft.

Plan 8

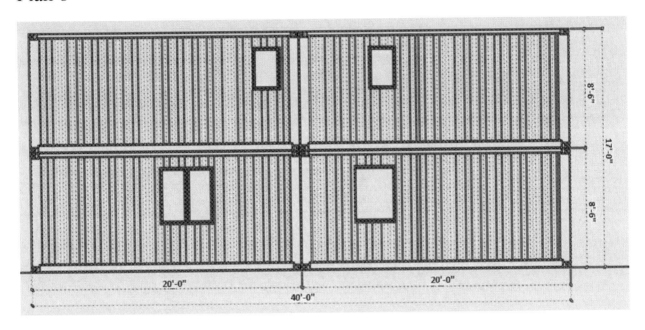

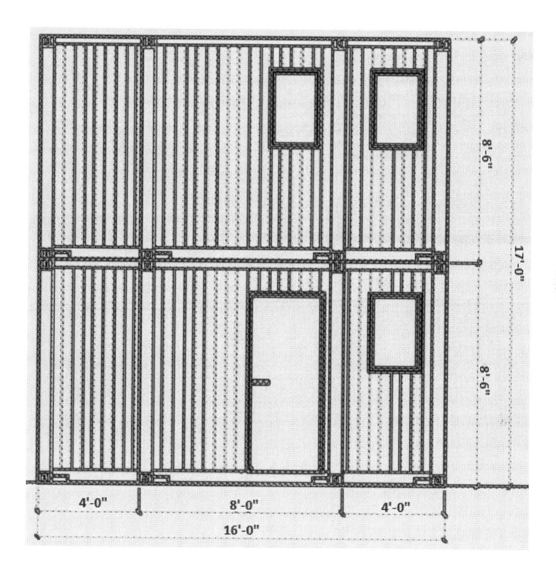

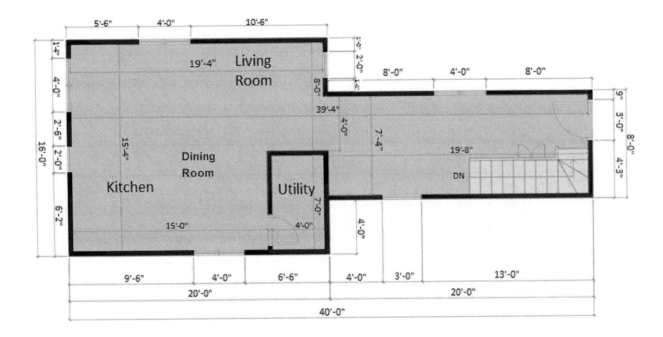

Upstairs:

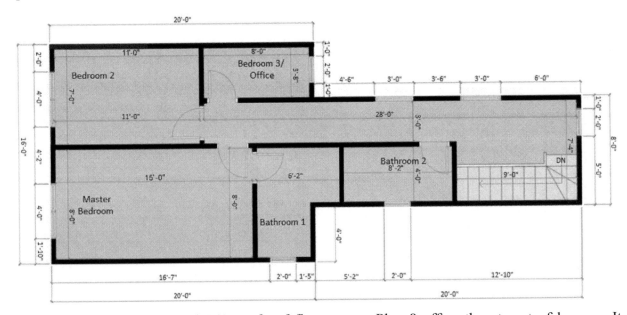

With six 20-ft. containers and 861 sq. ft. of floor space, Plan 8 offers the utmost of luxury. It features three bedrooms and two bathrooms on the upper floor, while the lower floor is devoted to a combined open-plan living room, dining room, and kitchen. Also included is a utility closet which serves your storage needs.

Plan 9

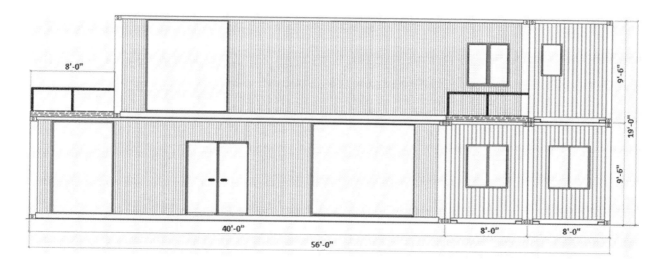

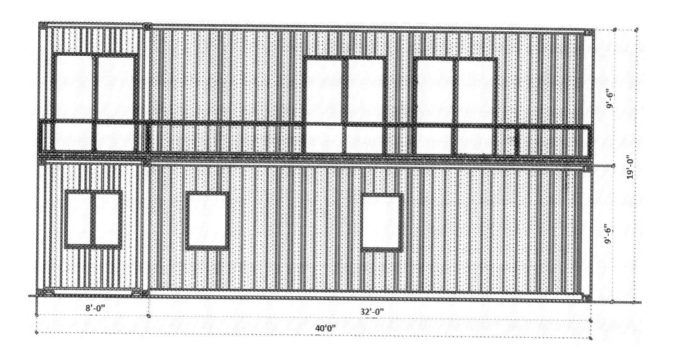

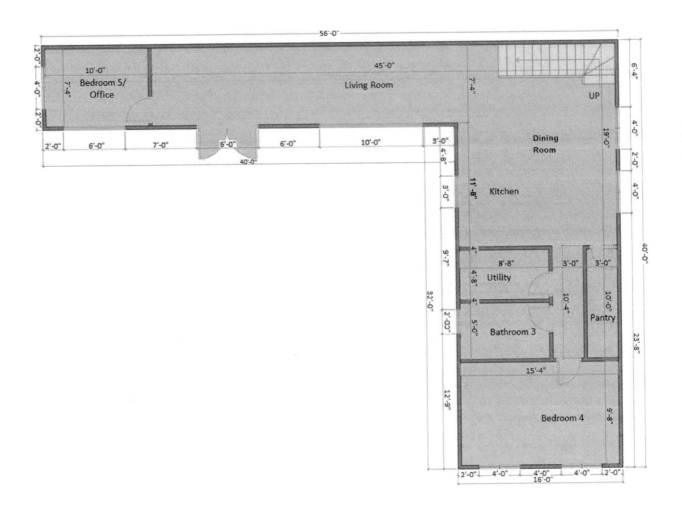

Upstairs:

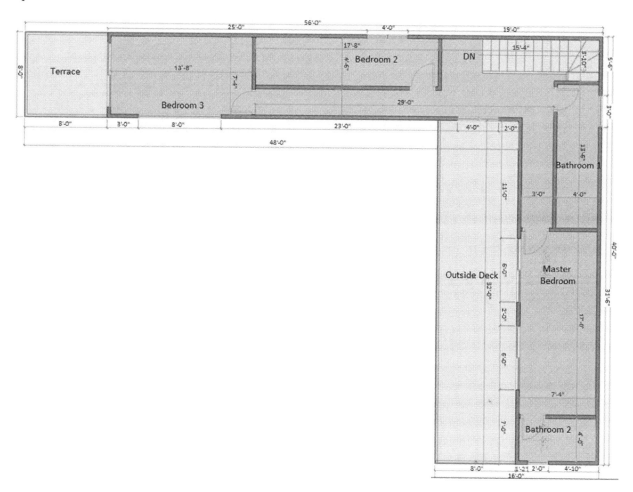

Plan 9 is composed of five 40-ft. high cube containers and provides a total of 1718 sq. ft. of floor space. It houses five bedrooms and three bathrooms as well as a combined kitchen and dining room. Also included are a pantry and utility closet. The second floor features an outside deck and terrace which are perfect for a combination of privacy and fresh air.

Plan 10

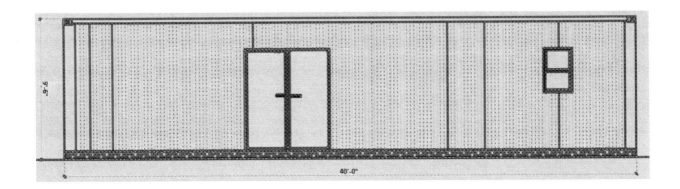

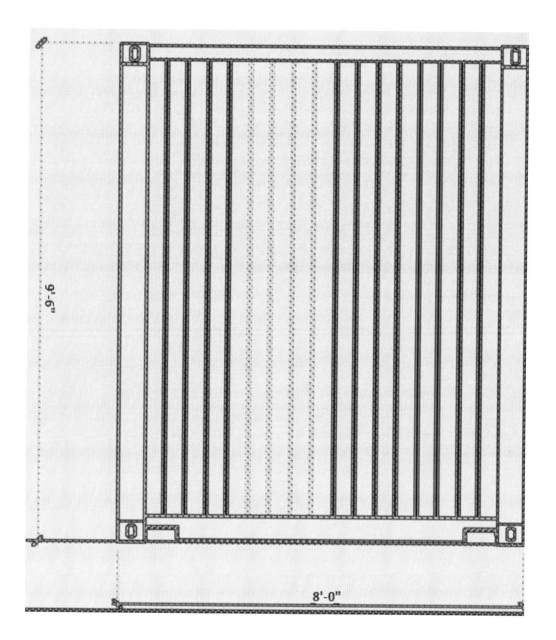

8'-0"

9'-6"

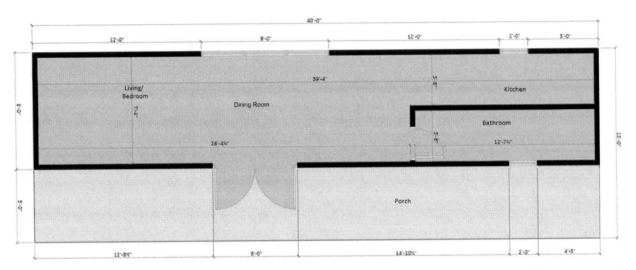

Constructed from a single 40-ft. container, Plan 10 offers a stunning 483 sq. ft. of floor space. It features a combined bedroom/living room and open-plan dining room, as well as a spacious bathroom and cozy kitchen. This design is ideal for two and can comfortably house three or more with a sofa bed.

Plan 11

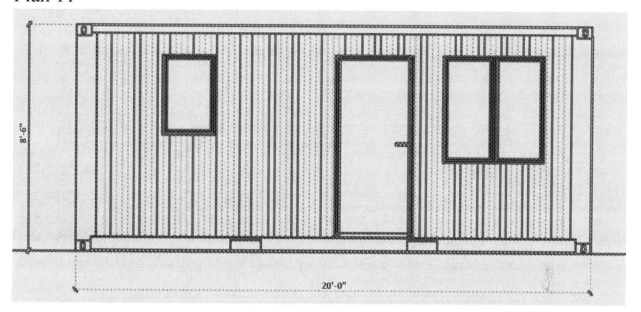

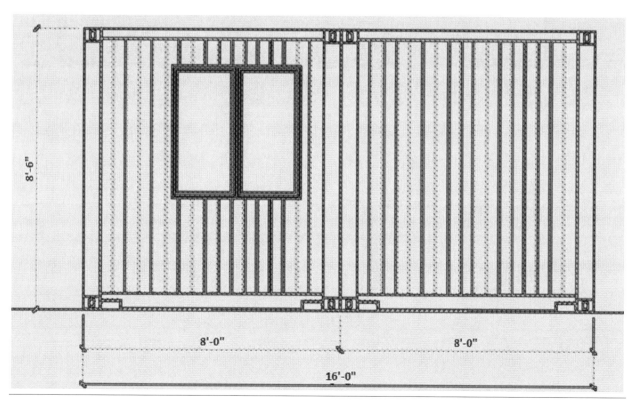

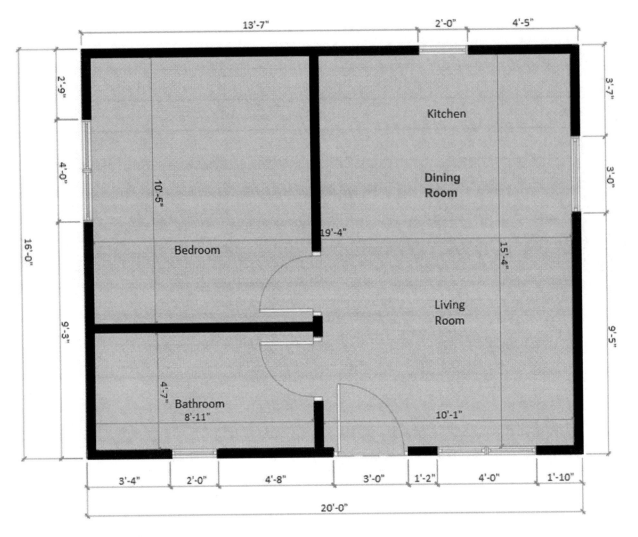

Made from only two 20-ft. containers, Plan 11 offers 289 sq. ft. of floor space. It features a master bedroom, luxurious bathroom, and combined kitchen and dining room. The front door opens into an open-plan living room which is ideal for visitors, and which can be supplied with a sofa bed to comfortably house a second person.

Plan 12

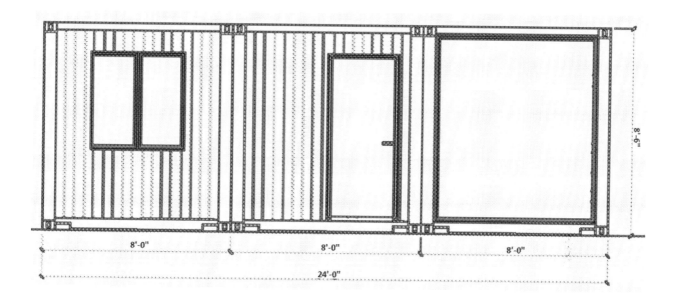

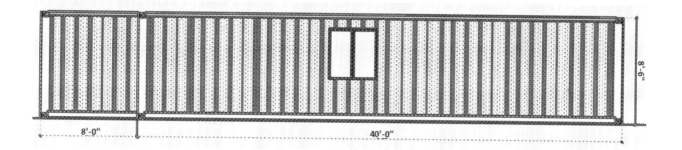

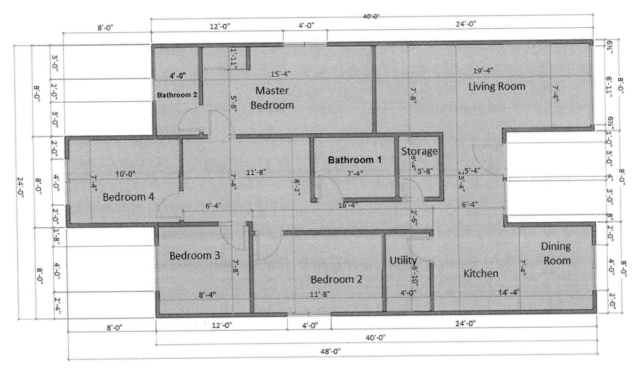

Constructed from merely three 40-ft. containers, Plan 12 offers a spacious 899 sq. ft. of floor space. It features a master bedroom as well as three additional bedrooms and two bathrooms. It also has an efficiently combined dining room and kitchen as well as a separate living room with ample space for entertaining visitors.

Planning Checklist

- Plan out the needs for your home.
- Set your budget.
- Meet with the local planning authorities to find the specifications and required paperwork for your area.
- Design your home.
- Obtain planning permission, if necessary.

Chapter 3 – Buying the Containers

After you have designed your shipping container home, it's time to source the containers. There are a number of options for sourcing, so here are some details to get familiar with the choices and know your way around the purchase. First, let's take a look at the dimensions of the containers.

The most common options will be the 20-ft. and 40-ft. containers, both of which come in both standard and high cube. High cube containers offer an additional foot of height, which can be helpful, especially if you plan to install a ceiling in your home. Here are tables which list the internal and external dimensions of each of these options:

External Dimensions

	Length	Width	Height
Standard 20 Foot	19'10 1/2" (6.06m)	8' (2.44m)	8'6" (2.59m)
Standard 40 Foot	40' (12.19m)	8' (2.44m)	8'6"(2.59m)
High Cube 20 Foot	19'10 1/2" (6.06m)	8' (2.44m)	9'6" (2.90m)
High Cube 40 Foot	40' (12.19m)	8' (2.44m)	9'6" (2.90m)

Internal Dimensions

	Length	Width	Height
Standard 20 Foot	19' 4 (5.89m)	7' 8 (2.34m)	7'10 (2.39m)
Standard 40 Foot	39' 5 (12.01m)	7' 8 (2.34m)	7'10 (2.39m)
High Cube 20 Foot	19' 4 (5.89m)	7' 8 (2.34m)	8'10 (2.69m)
High Cube 40 Foot	39' 5 (12.01m)	7' 8 (2.34m)	8'10 (2.69m)

Your best options will depend both upon the plans you've drawn up and the availability of containers in your local area, as shipping costs can be quite high if you purchase a container from an area far from your intended building site. Also, keep in mind that each manufacturer uses their own tolerance level for the dimension, so it's best to purchase all your containers from a single manufacturer.

New or Used?

One of the first decisions you will have to make when sourcing containers is if you wish to purchase new ones or those that have been in use. Also, you have a third option. You can purchase one-trip containers: these are used to ship cargo to its destination and then sold off once the cargo has been delivered. If you can find one-trip containers that suit your needs, this is an excellent option. They will be far cheaper than new containers without the wear and tear that is often found in used ones.

New and one-trip containers are easiest to work with, and they are generally in much better condition. You won't have to worry about rust, mold, or unknown chemical contamination. It is easier to build with them, and they tend to have a longer life expectancy.

Used containers are often exposed to pesticides or lead-based paints, so you may have an additional step in building your home and making it suitable for habitation. However, if you're working with a limited budget, you can definitely acquire used containers at a lower price. If you do decide to opt for a used container, here are some of the things you should look for before purchasing:

Leaks

This is a big one. You don't want a leaky home, and holes that allow water also create openings for other annoyances. Make sure to check the roof of the container and inspect the walls thoroughly. Also, smell the interior of the container to see if you get a hint of mold. This is another indication of possible leaks.

Rust

When purchasing a used container, you can expect a certain degree of light rusting. However, if there is rusting to such an extent as the integrity of the metal is compromised, find another container. Once again, it's important to check the roof as well when doing your inspection.

Functional Doors and Locks

Make sure to check the doors to ensure that they swing freely, and bolt them to make sure that they fasten securely and that the seal is intact.

Wooden Flooring in Good Repair

It's natural for a container to get a bit banged up when it's in use. However, you want to inspect the wooden flooring to make sure that there are no holes or breakages. Often, the original flooring is covered with a non-permeable layer and used as is, so you may have an additional, time-consuming step in construction if you unwittingly purchase a container with broken flooring.

Chemical Contamination

Here's where your nose will really come in handy. You want to smell for anything unusual. Containers may become exposed to pesticides or other chemical hazards when in use. Ask about the history of the container when purchasing, but do a little follow-up yourself to make sure you won't be exposing yourself and your family to chemicals.

Intact Identification Code

The shipping container identification code is an 11-digit alphanumeric code inscribed into the container. The history of a container can be tracked with this code, meaning that you can use it to see where it has been and what it has carried. Here is a sample Identification code:

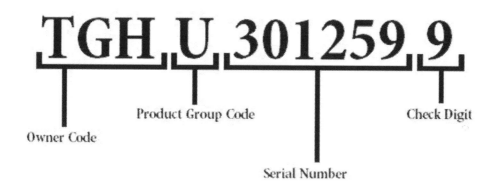

The first three digits, the owner code, identify the owner of the container. The fourth digit, the product group code, is a single letter. The only options for this digit are J, U, and Z. J indicates that there is equipment attached, while Z indicates a container trailer. If you are looking at a standard shipping container, you will see a U in this position. The remainder of the code is devoted to a six-digit serial number which indicates the precise container and a single number used as a check digit to verify the authenticity of the code. You can use this code to verify information about the container's history.

Where Can I Purchase It?

Shipping containers can be purchased from a number of sources. They are available in surplus all over the world. What you want to look for is a reputable dealer. These can be found easily with a Google search. Just search for "shipping container dealer" and add your location. This will yield a number of dealers in your area. Alternately, you can type "buy shipping container in …" and add your location. The search results should be similar if not identical.

One tool which helps those in search of shipping containers is the Green Cube Network. This is a search tool which helps to find shipping containers in your area. It's great for homing in on a list of dealers. Here is a link that will bring you straight to their search tool:

http://www.greencubenetwork.org/shipping-container-dealers_3/

If you're still having trouble, try out AliBaba, eBay, or Gumtree.

What's the Price?

The price will depend heavily on the supplier, the specific container, and the conditions of the deal. However, here are a few estimates that let you know if you're getting a good deal:

Dimensions		New			Used		
	U.S.(USD)	**Australia**(AUD)	**U.K.**(GBP)	U.S.	Australia	U.K.
20-ft. Standard	$3500	$4000	£2150	$2300	$2900	£1500
20-ft. High Cube	$3500	$4250	£2300	$2400	$3000	£1600
40-ft. Standard	$5900	$7400	£3800	$3000	$3800	£2000
40-ft. High Cube	$6000	$7700	£3900	$3100	$4000	£2100

A few additional considerations: When looking for your container, you're not just scouting for the best price. It's best to buy local for two reasons. First, you'll be able to inspect the container physically. This can save time and money and prevent you from making a purchase you'll regret later. Second, once you have purchased your container, you'll need it delivered. Longer journeys mean higher shipping costs, so the closer your container to the building site, the better for your budget.

Before shipping the container, you'll want to make sure you're ready to receive it. So, the next step is site preparation.

Container Purchasing Checklist
- Determine your budget for containers.

- Make any design adjustments necessary, factoring in the price of available containers.
- Decide on new, used, or one-time use containers.
- Source the containers from a reliable local supplier.
- If possible, inspect the container before purchase.

Chapter 4 – Site Preparation

The first step in preparing the site is exploring the soil type. You'll want to choose the foundation best suited for your site. There are a few options here, and the one you choose will depend upon the soil constitution of your building site.

The most common foundations used for shipping container homes are concrete piers, raft foundations, trench footings, and piles. However, to decide what's best for you, you need to know a bit about the strengths of each and the soil of your location. Some prefer to "over spec" their foundations, creating it to withstand forces stronger than will ever conceivably be required by the building. It's really up to you, once you have explored the options.

Soil Types

Dirt is just dirt, right? Wrong. There are many different soil types, and each holds a structural load differently. Here is a list of the soil types you may encounter in your building site and some of the construction aspects related to them:

Rock

If your building site is a slab of rock, it's actually a blessing. You need very little to build upon this, other than to ensure that it's level and strip the surface soil. This rock can consist of granite, schist, or diabase. It has a high load-bearing capacity and can hold anything you place upon it. One of the cheapest and easiest foundations to use in these conditions is the concrete pier foundation.

Gravel

We probably all know about gravel. It is coarse-grained material, easily dug out and offering excellent drainage. The best foundation for this type of soil is the trench footing.

Clay

Clay is extremely fine-grained and holds water. If your building site has a clay-based soil, you may be in for some costly preparation. You'll need to dig down until you find more stable soil. For this soil type, pile foundations or deep trench footings are most appropriate.

Sandy Soil

Sand consists of fine-grained particles, often containing a mix of gravel and rock. When working with these soils, it's important not to over-dig the foundation. This can increase the load on the softer soils below the layer of sand. The best foundation for this soil type is the raft foundation, often called a slab-on-grade.

What Soil Type Do I Have?

Unless you're a geotechnical engineer or the soil type is fairly obvious, it's best to seek out a bit of professional help for this stage of the game. The geotechnical engineer will explore the entire site, doing soil borings to evaluate the soil constitution at different depths. This will give you a solid and comprehensive idea of what you're working with and the best foundation to support your dwelling.

Typically, a soil engineer will perform test bores across the site, spaced 100 to 150 ft. apart. These test bearings will supply a soil profile, providing an indication of the load-bearable soil. These tests will indicate water content, density, and particle size of the soil, as well as the soil classification, depth of different soil types, and ground water level of your site. Bores will be continued into at least 20 ft. of load-bearing soil.

Geotechnical engineers will also explore the surface qualities of the soil, identifying soils which challenge the building process. They will explore the elevation of the site, offering indications as to how the site can be leveled most effectively. In essence, the geotechnical engineer will provide a report which indicates:

- ✓ Surface soil type
- ✓ Subsurface soil type
- ✓ Soil bearing capacity
- ✓ Groundwater depth
- ✓ Frost depth

- ✓ Soil compaction
- ✓ Recommended foundation type
- ✓ Recommended foundation depth
- ✓ Drainage requirements

Tip: Sometimes the local authority has information on the soil profile of your area. If you plan to build within city limits, this is a high likelihood. If you are building something a bit further out, you can almost guarantee that a soil profile will be necessary, and should factor this into your budget.

Foundation Type

We've already explored the four foundation types that you will need to know about when preparing your site. They are: concrete piers, raft foundations, trench footings, and pile foundations. Here are a few structural and geotechnical details about each foundation to help you select the one right for your shipping container home. Also included are all the details you'll need to plan and lay the foundation of your home. This being said, it's important to meet with a structural engineer to make sure that your foundation can hold the necessary load, and that it's designed to the specifications you need.

Concrete Piers

Essentially, concrete piers are steel-reinforced concrete cubes laid out at the corners and load-bearing center of your structure. For a single container, you will need six of these cubes, one at each corner and two to support the outer walls at the center of your structure. They offer a shallow foundation and are both cheap and DIY-friendly. Additional benefits include the fact that the container will be elevated off the soil with this foundation type, reducing the need for insulation, allowing ventilation, and reducing the buildup of condensation on the floor of the container.

Below is a diagram which indicates the placement of the piers:

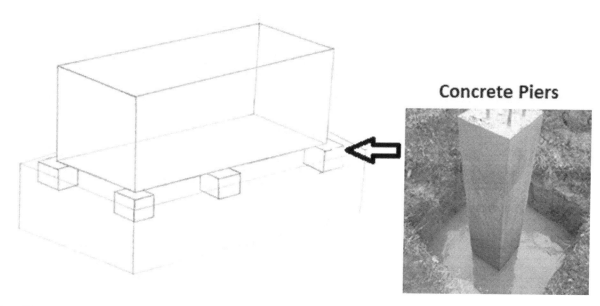

Concrete Piers

Laying Your Concrete Pier Foundation

The first step in laying your foundation is to determine the placement of the corners. This is a set of instructions which offers step-by-step details on how to plot out and lay the foundation for a 40-ft. container.

Begin with one corner and drive a 2 in. x 2 in. 1-ft. stake 6 in. into the ground.

Nail a 40-ft. string into the top of the first stake, and then use this first stake as a marker to measure 40 ft. to the second corner. Nail a second stake into the ground, just as you have done the first. You have now marked out the length of your container.

Attach a 40-ft., 9.5 in. string to one stake and another 8-ft. string to the other. Ensuring that both strings are taut, find their intersection point. This is the third corner of your container. Nail another stake into this point.

Repeat step three to determine the final corner of your container.

Run a line between two of the corners of your container, lengthwise.

Use a tape measure to determine the point 20 ft. along this line from one corner.

Repeat step 6 to find the point along the length of your container on the other side.

Once you have marked out the placement of the piers, dig a hole 50cm deep, 50cm wide, and 50cm long (50cm is about 2 ft., 4 in.).

Place a form around the hole. You may choose to use pre-made concrete forms at this time. Sonotubes© work extremely well for this purpose. If you are creating the form on your own, 1.5mm plastic lining will do the trick.

Once you have placed the form, line the space of the pier with rebar in a grid formation. Try to ensure that you place three across the length and three across the width, binding the rebar together with steel wire. Repeat this pattern vertically every 6 in.

Drive three reinforced metal bars through the foot of the pier vertically, using these to stabilize each horizontal level of rebar reinforcement. Tie each horizontal level in to these bars.

Fill these holes with concrete.

Allow the concrete to cure for a minimum of seven days before placement. (More details on curing concrete and selecting the appropriate concrete for your foundation can be found below.)

Offered below are a few diagrams which illustrate the measuring and laying of the concrete pier foundation.

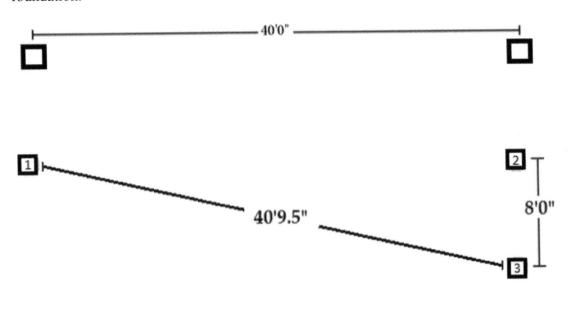

Measuring Out the Corners

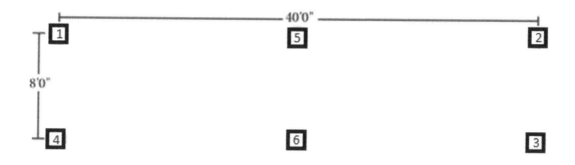

Reinforcing the Piers

Seeing the Piers in Action

Piling Foundation

Essentially, pile foundations are exactly the same as pier foundations. The only difference is that they are driven deeper into the ground. They are best for moving past unsuitable soils and driving into a soil type more capable of bearing a load. The measurement is the same; however, in order to drive the piles, you will likely need specialized equipment. Therefore, this is one of the most expensive options.

Piles are cylindrical steel tubes which are driven into the ground until they reach a suitable soil depth. Once the piles reach a soil capable of bearing a load, they are filled with concrete. Above ground, a pile foundation looks very similar to a pier foundation. In order to lay a pile foundation, you will need to contract a pile driver and purchase the cylinders to house the piles. This makes it one of the less desirable foundation types for a DIY build; however, it can be an indispensable option when dealing with more troublesome soil types.

Offered below are a couple of diagrams which demonstrate the pile foundation in action:

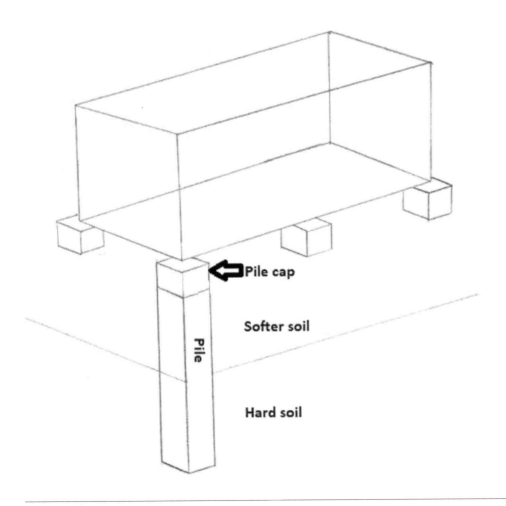

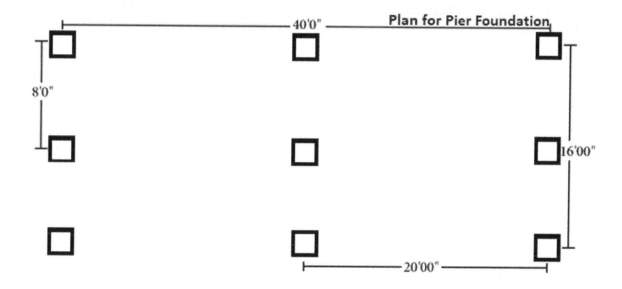

Plan for Pier Foundation

Raft Foundation

This foundation type is often known in the construction industry as slab-on-grade. Essentially, it involves leveling a space of ground, digging down to the required depth, and then placing a layer of concrete which will support the entire length and width of your structure.

The slab-on-grade is more costly in terms of time and resources than the trench foundation or concrete pier; however, it is ideal for sandy and loose soils. It essentially creates a structure which floats above unstable material, offering a solid foundation on loose soils without requiring you to dig down to a solid subgrade. When your soil type is unsuitable for a great depth, the slab-on-grade offers an elegant solution which does not require the heavy machinery costs of a pile-driver.

Although the raft foundation is excellent for softer soils, it does offer a number of disadvantages. First, it can be a source of heat loss in colder climates. With the container seated right against the concrete, heat escapes easily. Therefore, you will need a thick layer of insulation on the lower surface and floor of the container. Second, as mentioned before, you'll have to dig quite a bit to prepare the soil for a slab-on-grade. Finally, you'll have to place the utilities before you pour, and you will not have external access to the lines once the concrete has hardened.

Despite these disadvantages, the slab-on-grade foundation offers a great degree of stability, and the lack of space between container and foundation makes it less susceptible to pests like termites.

Typically, with a raft foundation, you will want to give a depth of 2 ft. below your desired elevation and extend 2 ft. beyond the edges of your structure. These requirements will vary with soil type and with the special conditions of your site. Offered below is a diagram which provides a visual of the raft foundation both before and after a structure has been placed upon it.

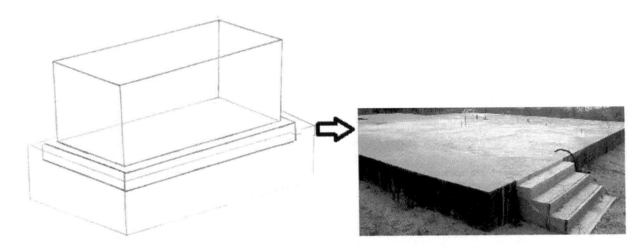

Important: If using a slab-on-grade foundation, make sure that your utilities are placed before pouring. Otherwise, you will be unable to access the area necessary to place your lines.

Trench Foundation

The trench foundation is also known as the spread footing or strip foundation. Essentially, it combines the qualities of the pier and raft foundation, providing a solid foundation beneath the entire edge of the structure. With all of the container's exterior walls supported, the weight is distributed over a larger area than with the pier or piling foundations.

Areas of poor drainage can be benefited by using a variant of this foundation known as the "rubble trench." If you place a layer of gravel or loose stone beneath the concrete base, then water is allowed to escape while the load of the structure is held secure.

The diagram below demonstrates the appropriate placement of the trench foundation:

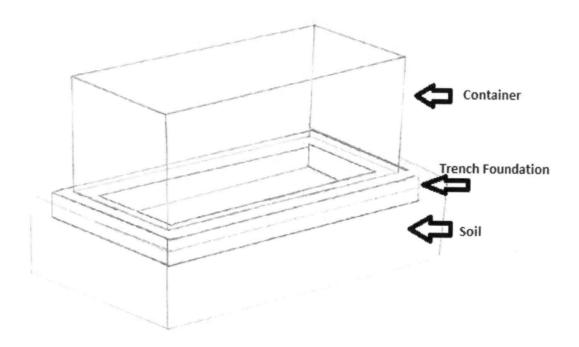

A few notes: The trench, pier, and raft foundations require a minimum of 50cm of depth. You will also want to ensure that both trench and raft foundations extend at least a foot beyond the edge of the structure. For the trench foundation, ensure that the inner edge of the footing also extends inwardly at least a foot past the inner edge of the structure.

Preparing and Placing Your Concrete

Concrete is a beautiful building material to work with, offering a potential to be formed into any shape desired and a high compressive strength. However, there are a few things to be aware of in order to make sure that you can place it effectively and ensure it cures to the desired strength.

First, a few things about what concrete actually is: Concrete is a combination between cement, gravel, and sand. When cement mixes with water, a chemical reaction ensues. The cement hardens as the water evaporates, trapping the sand and gravel within the matrix of the hardened cement. This combination offers a high degree of compressive strength. In other words, it can take quite a bit of pressure without a loss of integrity. The process of water evaporation and chemical hardening is called "curing," and is the process whereby concrete attains its full compressive strength.

The strength of your concrete depends upon the ratio of cement to aggregate. The final strength of a concrete mix is indicated in ready-mixes by a C-value. All-purpose concrete has a strength of C-15 and utilizes a mix of one part cement to two parts sand and five parts gravel. To create concrete with a strength of C-30, simply combine one part cement to two parts sand and three parts gravel.

The report of the geotechnical engineer will determine the necessary strength of concrete for your foundation.

Small quantities of concrete can be mixed by hand or with a cement mixer. For anything larger than one cubic meter, it may be more efficient to have the concrete delivered to the site. If mixing the elements by hand ensure that they are thoroughly combined, otherwise the strength of the resulting concrete will suffer.

Calculating the necessary volume of concrete is a simple matter of determining the volume of your desired placement. The one thing to remember is that concrete volume is calculated in cubic meters. Here are a few sample calculations for a single 40-ft. container to help you get the idea:

Pier Foundations: $6 \times (50cm)^3 = 6 \times 125,000cm^3 = 750,000cm^3$

$1,000,000cm^3 = 1m^3 \rightarrow 750,000cm^3 = .75m^3$

Raft Foundation: $(40+2)ft \times (8+2)ft \times 2ft = 840ft^3$

$1ft^3 = .283m^3 \rightarrow 840ft^3 = 23.72m^3$

Trench Foundation: $(40+2)ft \times 2ft \times 2ft + (8-2)ft \times 2ft \times 2ft \rightarrow 168ft^3 + 24ft^3 \rightarrow 192ft^3$

$1ft^3 = .283m^3 \rightarrow 192ft^3 = 5.44m^3$

It might take just a little bit of math to get there, but with a small amount of planning, you'll know exactly how much concrete you'll need.

Give your concrete five to seven days after placement to cure to full strength. If you're placing concrete in warm weather, moisten the soil with cold water before you pour, mix the cement with cold water, and shade the concrete after placement. You can also place the concrete in late evening or early morning to avoid high heat during the most sensitive curing times.

If pouring in extreme cold, make sure to clear any snow, ice, or standing water before placing the concrete. Cover the concrete with insulating blankets once it has been placed. Once the concrete has cured, remove the blankets gradually to prevent cracking from rapid changes in temperature.

Tip: Another option is to place a steel plate upon the corners of the foundation before the concrete sets. This will increase the strength of your foundation and allow you to weld the container securely to it.

Site Preparation Checklist

- Get a geoengineering soil profile.

- Determine the most appropriate foundation type and depth.
- Meet with a structural engineer to design the foundation.
- Decide if you can pour the foundation yourself or if you need a contractor. If you do need a contractor for the job, hire well.
- Calculate the concrete strength required for the job.
- Calculate the volume of concrete required to pour the foundation.
- Dig the foundation.
- Place the molds.
- Place a grid work of rebar and steel wire into the molds to reinforce and offer flexural stability to the concrete once it has cured.
- Mix concrete to the necessary strength and pour into the molds, ensuring that the foundation is level.
- Pour with your weather conditions in mind, ensuring that the concrete is able to maintain a stable temperature as it cures.
- Allow the concrete to cure for five to seven days before placement.

Chapter 5 – Container Conversion, Delivery, and Placement

Now that we've addressed obtaining your container and preparing the site, it's time to look into shipping the container to your desired building site. An important factor to consider here is whether you'll be making the necessary modifications to convert your container to a dwelling onsite or if the conversion will be done elsewhere.

Other important considerations include the budget for shipping new, used, or one-time use containers and the location from which they are being shipped. We'll take all of these considerations in turn with the sections that follow.

Converting Your Container – On or Offsite?

Converting your container means making the necessary modifications to create the shell of your living space. Certain designs require walls to be removed so that containers can be connected to create larger spaces. Doorways, arches, and windows must also be cut through the steel. Some of these modifications will require equipment, such as welding tools, cutting torches, grinders, heavy-duty drills, and sprayers for insulation. Sometimes, it is more economical to have the containers delivered to a workshop supplied with the necessary tools.

On the other hand, having the containers delivered directly to the site and making the modifications in place can save you an additional shipping cost. The catch is that you need access to the necessary tools and skills to make this option work for you. Here is a breakdown of the pros and cons of onsite and offsite conversion, as well as a third option which might serve you:

Onsite Conversion

If you can manage the conversion onsite, it is helpful for a number of reasons. The first is that you will have uninterrupted access to the site. You can make your own hours when converting your shipping container to a home. And, perhaps worthy of mentioning first, once you have converted your container, it is already in place and won't require any further travel.

Converting the containers compromises their structural integrity to a certain degree. This isn't an issue if they are already in place; however, if they are converted offsite, then you will have to be doubly careful in transit. Onsite conversion avoids this issue altogether.

There are a few challenges associated with onsite conversion. First, you'll need to have the tools and skills to do the conversion in place. If you intend to purchase the tools specifically for this job, this can be an expensive option. Plus, if you're building on a green field site, you'll need to supply power and water. This often means a generator, which can be noisy and expensive. You can also choose to have electric facilities established before placement, though this will have to be planned out ahead of time.

One option that is available to you if you choose to convert your containers in place is to contract a construction team for the conversion process. This sidesteps the need to buy costly tools and makes sure that you have the necessary skills at hand to make the conversion. However, it is a more expensive option than a DIY project. This is an ideal option if you lack the necessary tools and skill and if it is unfeasible to station your containers at a local workshop in order to convert them.

A third option is to have your containers converted prior to delivery. This will be more expensive than either of the previous options; however, you will be able to save quite a bit of time and place your containers directly once they are delivered. Purchasing your containers pre-converted will also ensure that they are both modified and delivered professionally, and that they make their way into place intact and without damage.

Offsite Conversion

If you aren't well supplied with tools, then one good option is to have the containers delivered to a local workshop or fabricator. Once they are delivered, you can use the tools supplied there to make all necessary modifications before transporting them to your building site. In addition to the tools, you'll have a number of experienced people on hand that can help you with any details that require a bit more know-how.

One big advantage is that workshops provide protection from the rain and the elements. You won't have to worry about making sure your containers are watertight immediately. They will also be protected overnight, so you won't have to worry about tampering or interference when you are unable to be onsite. Finally, while at a workshop, you will have access to water and power, which means you won't have to set up supplies prior to delivery.

Although offsite modification offers a number of advantages, there are also a few disadvantages to consider. First, the location of the workshop might be fairly distant from you, requiring a hefty commute to and from it to work on the modifications. Second, the workshop is unlikely to be open at all hours. This means that you may find yourself limited in your access to the container, especially if you are working a regular job in the process. Look into the times that the workshop or fabricator will be open before deciding to use it for your modifications, and try to arrange a flat fee for the month or the week if possible.

Container Delivery

Once you have decided how to modify your container and made all necessary site preparations, it's time to nail down the details for container delivery. You already know where your container is going. How is it going to get there?

Local dealers offer a number of advantages in this respect. First and foremost, most local dealers operate in conjunction with a freight service that can handle delivery. Furthermore, they can help to ensure that all the containers you purchase come from the same company. This helps to avoid differences in tolerance with regard to internal and external dimensions. Despite this, you can sometimes cut costs by contracting an external freight service. In order to get the best deal, you'll have to shop around and explore your options.

New Containers

If you are purchasing your containers new, they will cost a bit more, but they are sure to come in good condition. However, you will want to seek out a supplier relatively close to you, otherwise you may end up paying as much for the shipping as you do for the containers themselves. Shipping your containers new requires you to pay the full delivery cost. However, opting for the one-time use ensures that you get good-as-new containers and that the bulk of the shipping cost is paid by the company receiving their cargo.

Just to give you an idea of the importance of this decision, shipping new containers from a remote location like China may cost anywhere from $2000 – $23,000 USD, just to have them arrive at a nearby port. On the other hand, if you select a one-time use container, you can have them arrive at no cost to yourself. The only thing to factor in to your budget is the cost of getting the containers from the port to the building site.

Shipping Costs

As indicated above, shipping costs will vary greatly depending upon the origin of the container. Some estimates include $230 USD to transport a 20-ft. container 50 miles and offloading it, $420

USD for a similar delivery of a 40-ft. container, and $400 USD for a 300-mile transportation of 20-ft. containers. Clearly, this will depend upon the shipping company, the number of containers, and the conditions surrounding their journey.

One thing to remember is to make sure that you have arranged the containers with plenty of time for delivery. Shipping companies sometimes need from weeks to months to make a delivery, depending upon their distance. Also, they most frequently deal in bulk, so the few shipping containers you need to build your home won't be their highest priority. Try to make the arrangements early so that the containers will arrive when your site is prepared and ready for modification.

Another tip that can save you quite a bit of money is to remember to shop around. The shipping costs can differ quite a bit from one company to another, so if you explore a number of options, you can make sure to get the best price given your circumstances.

Placing Your Container

Tilting the Container Into Place

Once your container reaches the site, there are a few options for placing it. The cheapest option is for the container to be delivered on a flatbed trailer. If the site allows, you may be able to have the driver tilt the bed and slide the container directly onto the foundation. This is also the easiest way to go, and if you can plan your design and site layout to make it a possibility, then you will be able to save the price of renting either a crane or HIAB. In order to do this, you will need to arrange the foundation so that there is the space of a flatbed trailer and truck adjacent to the narrow end of the foundation, leaving space for the truck to maneuver.

Placing With Crane or HIAB

Sometimes, tilting the container onto the foundation is simply not an option. Also, the tilting option is unfeasible if your construction is more complicated or multi-level. If this is the case, then you will need to lift your container(s) and set it upon the foundation. A HIAB is cheaper, and it will work for smaller containers; however, it may be unable to lift anything more than a 20-ft. container. A crane, though more expensive, will have sufficient lifting power and control for heavier containers and more delicate operations. The typical price for crane rental is $700 USD per day, though this will depend upon the contractor.

Lining and Insulation

One important tip when placing your containers upon the foundation is to line them with polyethylene damp-proof membrane. Also, if you use a crane or HIAB, you will have access to the underside of the containers. You can lift them one by one, sandblast the bottom, and add a 1 in. coating of polyurethane spray-foam insulation. This will reduce heat loss from the bottom of the container. Even without the benefit of a crane or HIAB, you can treat the underside of the container if using a concrete pier foundation.

Tip: If your foundation isn't completely level, you may need to use shims, metal spacers, to raise the container and bring it level.

Tip: By spraying foam insulation between any connecting walls once the containers have been lined up, you can keep moisture out, reduce drafts, and help maintain the internal temperature of the containers.

Stabilizing Your Containers

Cleaning the Containers
Once you have placed your containers, you'll begin to see the shell of your home shaping up. The next step is to connect them. First, however, they will need to be thoroughly cleaned. This will be more important for used containers than new or one-time use. The sand blaster and pressure washer are the quickest options for cleaning; however, in a pinch, you can use a grinder or even wire wool. Make sure to clean the inside of the container, including the wooden flooring. Then proceed to the outer walls and roof of the container.

Stabilizing the Containers on the Foundation
In most cases, the weight of the container alone will be sufficient to seat the container firmly upon the foundation. However, if you have chosen to place steel plates into the surface of the concrete on the corners of the foundation, the containers can be welded to the plates to stabilize them further.

Another option is to bolt the containers to the foundation. In order to do this, you will want to drill through the bottom corner fittings of the container into the piers, piles, trench, or slab. Once the hole has been drilled, you can place a 12-in. by 1-in. bolt through the hole. Make sure that you use a washer around the head of the bolt to seat it firmly to the bottom of the container. Then hammer the bolt into the hole you have drilled. To achieve the final snug, tighten the head of the bolt. You will only need one bolt in the corner of each container to ensure that they are solid and secure.

Connecting the Containers
Once the containers have been placed and bolted or welded to the foundation, it's time to connect them securely to one another. You have three options at this point: bolt, weld, or clamp.

Clamping

The least secure (and least expensive) of the three is to clamp the containers together. It does offer the option of disconnecting the containers from one another in the future, should that be desired. However, given that they have already been bolted securely in place, other options should be used if at all possible.

Bolting

Bolting the containers together is the next option. It is more secure than clamping and only slightly more expensive. If you opt for this option, the containers should be bolted together at the adjacent corners. Drill through the corner fitting points from one container to the next. You will also want to drill through a metal plate. This will act as a washer for the threaded side of the bolt. Insert the bolt through the hole (including a washer), slide it through the containers, and then place the metal plate, an additional washer, and a nut on the threaded end. Torque the nut tight, and then seal any gaps by placing mastic around both ends of the bolt.

Welding

Like clamping, bolting leaves the option of disassembling the containers later should the need require. However, the best option by far is welding. Welding makes the overall structure more rigid and secure. It also helps to keep the containers level despite settling. If you have access to the equipment and tools, then welding is by far the best option for a long-lasting shipping container home with a minimum of repairs needed over its lifetime.

The containers should be welded at the jointure of the roof, floor, and end walls. One of the best methods is to place a 3-in. x 1/8-in. length of flat steel against the jointure of the roofs and secure it with a stitch weld. Once this has been welded in place, repeat the process for each end wall with a 2-in. x 1/8-in. length of flat steel. Finally, use another 2-in. x 1/8-in. piece of flat steel to weld together any overlapping floors of adjoining containers. This will ensure that all of the contact points between containers are welded securely to one another.

Tip: To prevent rust, place a few layers of latex paint over each of the flat steel bars. Make sure to completely cover the area of the weld.

Conversion Plan, Delivery, Placement, and Connection Checklist

- Shop around to get a number of quotes for container shipping.
- Decide whether to convert the containers onsite or offsite, and plan your delivery accordingly.
- Arrange container delivery.

- Explore the site and design to determine whether crane, flatbed, or HIAB are most appropriate for placement.
- If possible, insulate the bottoms of the containers prior to placement.
- After placing the containers, secure them to the foundation with bolts or welds.
- Spray foam insulation between adjoining walls.
- Connect the containers securely to one another with clamps, bolts, or welds.

Chapter 6 – Fitting the Roof

Building a roof onto your shipping container home is a matter of preference. The easiest solution is to use the flat roof, the roof of the container itself. While this will save quite a bit on both construction costs and time, it does leave your container susceptible to pooling and rust.

The flat roof also offers very little insulation. Since heat rises, most of the heat will be lost from the top. To top it off, the container itself is made out of steel. It will collect both heat and cold and transfer it to the interior. Without insulation, you could be paying an arm and a leg in heating and cooling during more extreme weather.

Other options for roofing will help to add additional insulation, provide a layer of protection from pooling water, and offer overhangs to keep water from dripping down the windows. Some alternatives for roofing styles are the shed roof and the gable roof. The construction methods for each style are explored below, along with a discussion of the benefits of each.

Roofing Styles

Flat Roof

As mentioned above, the flat roof is the easiest, quickest, and cheapest option. It requires little to no modification, as you are simply using the metal roof of the container. This option will be more than sufficient for most purposes. However, there are certain measures which should be taken to ensure the longevity and comfort of your dwelling.

The drawbacks of a flat roof have been addressed above. The first is pooling of water on the roof from rain. This can lead to rust and to the loss of structural integrity. One easy solution is to place a tarpaulin over the roof of the container. This can then be covered with rolls of asphalt. This will weigh the tarpaulin in place and offer an additional layer of defense against the elements.

The asphalt will then need to be fixed into place. When covering the roof of the container, make sure to leave an overhang of at least 2 in. You can then bolt 2-in. x 1/8-in. steel bar into the top of the container through the asphalt. Make sure to seal the bolt-holes with mastic so that you don't have leakage during heavy rains.

Before installing your tarpaulin and asphalt protective layer, you may choose to cover the roof with a 1-in. thick layer of spray foam. This will offer a certain degree of insulation; however, you will want to add to this by installing a ceiling and insulating this as well. Construction details for ceiling installation and insulation are offered in Chapters 7 and 9.

Offered below is a simple diagram which demonstrates the flat roof option for your shipping container home:

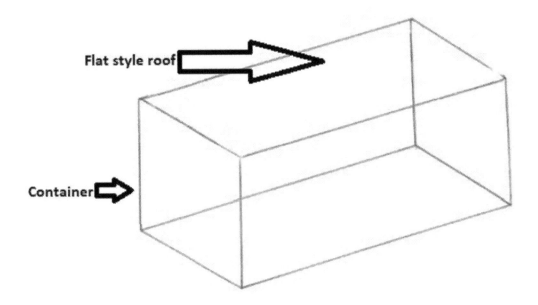

Shed Roof

The shed roof is essentially a single slope, angled downward from one end of your structure to the other. This is a cheap construction and easy to build, taking days or less from initial construction to completion. Another benefit to this option is that it is ideal for housing solar panels. This requires a bit more in the way of tools, resources, and know-how, but is the cheapest and simplest option if you choose to add a built roof to your home.

Offered below is a simple diagram which shows the basic design of the shed roof:

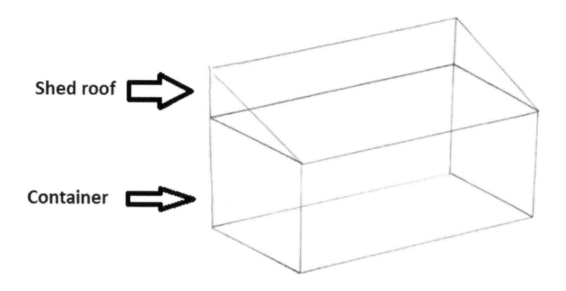

Installation

The first step in installing a shed roof is to weld right-angled steel plates to the length of the shipping container on both sides. Once this has been done, the next step is to afix a wooden beam to the raised flange of the plate: 2x6 beams are suitable for this purpose, and will be used to nail the trusses into place. Place the trusses about 18 in. apart. This means that you will need about 14 trusses for a 20-ft. container and about 28 for a 40-ft. container.

When securing the trusses, make sure that you use a skew nailing technique. This involves hammering two nails into the truss at each point, 25 degrees either way from the vertical. This creates an x-shape which holds the trusses solidly in place under lateral pressure.

Once the trusses have been secured, the basic shape of the roof will be visible. The next step is to line the angle of the trusses with 20 ft.-long purlins, beams which create the horizontal surface across the angle of the trusses. The purlins should be placed about 1 ft. apart. Next, brace the trusses to protect against pressure which comes from windforce. The diagram below shows the initial stage of a shed-style roof construction:

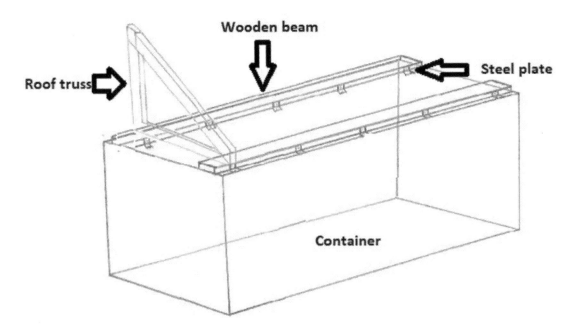

Wooden beam

Roof truss

Steel plate

Container

The final step in the construction of your shed-style roof is to cover it. This can be done in a number of ways. Your options include the use of shingles, coated steel sheets, or galvanized steel sheets. Shingles will be the cheapest option; however, it is also the least durable. Galvanized metal sheets are more durable, as well as being quite easy to fit.

The most durable option is coated steel, though this will be a bit more expensive and require more in terms of tools and know-how. If you're looking for the maximum longevity of your construction, regardless of the cost, this is the option you'll want to choose. Explore the options, in terms of finances, skills, budget, and timing, and you'll have the best idea as to which roof covering will be best for you.

The final step in the construction of the shed roof is to ensure that it has sufficient ventilation. In order to do this effectively, you must first make sure that the trusses overhang the roof by 1 ft. on both sides. Affix a fascia board to both lengths of the roof, and then install a soffit board with a gap of 1 in. for ventilation. Wire mesh should cover the ventilation gap to allow airflow while preventing pests. Ventilation will allow air to flow freely through the entire structure of the roof. This avoids both heat-traps and rust-causing condensation.

Tips: Make sure to check your design with a structural engineer. They will be able to determine the exact load-bearing requirements of your roof, given the natural stresses imposed by wind, rain, and snow in your region. The number of trusses and purlin placement have been offered as an over spec recommendation, fitting for most circumstances.

The diagram below shows the construction of the fascia and soffit board:

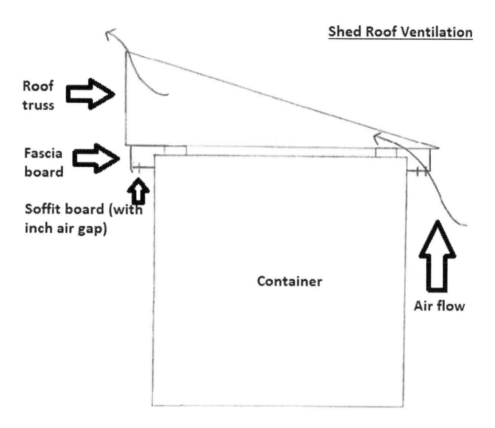

Gable Roof

The next option for roofing style is the gable roof. Gable roofs are peaked in the center and slope down to each edge of the length of the dwelling. This is a more traditional roof, offering a more aesthetic finish to the dwelling and resembling the roof of a traditional home. It offers a triangular roof which is ideal for water draining, thus improving longevity of both your roof and your dwelling. Another advantage is that the gabled roof offers a great deal more ceiling space than other roof styles. For most designs, this will not be an issue in shipping container homes; however, it does offer the opportunity to line your roof with more insulation.

The diagram below shows the general design of the gable roof:

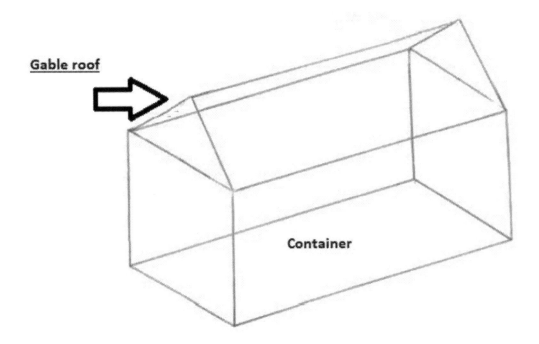

Gable roof

Container

Installation

The installation of the gable roof is similar to that of the shed roof installation. The first step, just as in that of the shed-style roof installation, is to weld a right-angled steel play across both lengths of the container. Once again, the upper flange of the right-angled plate is then used as a base to affix wooden 2x6 beams. Screw or nail the trusses into place using a skew pattern, and place the trusses about 18 in. apart. Affix the purlins with nails or screws, placing them approximately 1 ft. apart. Shingles, galvanized steel plates, or coated steel sheets can be used to cover the purlins.

Once again, in providing sufficient ventilation, ensure that the trusses overhang the width of the roof by 1 ft. on each side. Install fascia and soffit boards, providing a 1 in. gap in the center of the soffit boards to allow for airflow, and cover these gaps with wire mesh. The diagrams below show the construction cross-section of the gable roof and the details which show how to arrange appropriate ventilation:

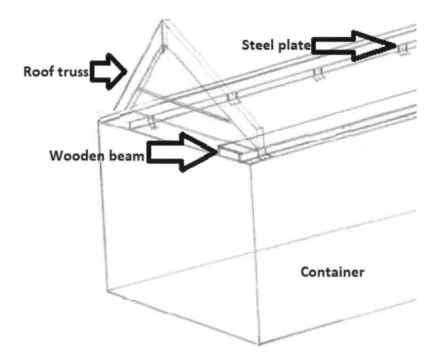

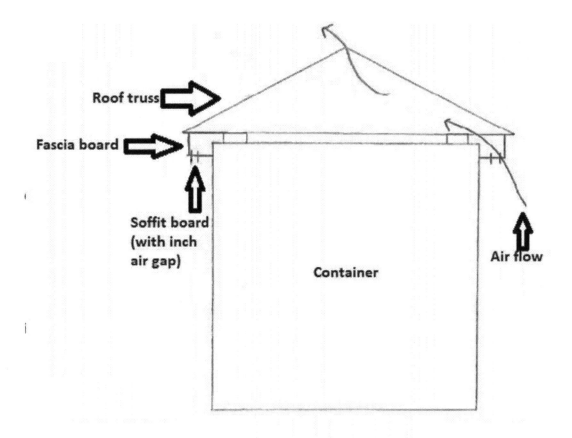

Labels in figure: Roof truss, Fascia board, Soffit board (with inch air gap), Container, Air flow

Roofing Checklist

- Consult with a structural engineer about the roofing and load-bearing needs of your home. Take the load-bearing requirements into consideration for your area and the typical weather patterns.
- Decide upon the roofing style for your home.
- Construct your roof.

Chapter 7 – First Fix Services: Water, Electricity, Sewage, Phone Line

No home is complete without basic services. First fix services involve running the lines for electricity, telephone, sewage, and water into your container. For water, this essentially involves running the main, while sewage involves attaching the drain point(s) and running the line to the sewer or septic tank. With telephone and electricity, the lines are run to the outside of the container and led through the service box into the interior.

Once the first fix services have been established, it will be necessary to take care of flooring, framing the ceiling and interior walls, and placing the insulation. The second-fix services can be placed to ensure that the service lines are run to their desired location in the completed home. This involves light fixtures, light switches, interior electric boxes, faucets, and any other services which must be run through the interior of the home.

Choices with regard to services should be made with consideration of the chosen foundation type. It's important to remember that if you choose a raft or trench foundation, you will need to lay out the lines for water, electricity, sewage, and phone before you lay the foundation. You have a bit more leeway if you choose a pier or pile foundation, as you can run the lines for services after placing the container.

In order to have access to the underground lines for sewage and water, you will need to remove a portion of the flooring. This will not be necessary for electricity and telephone lines, as they can be led into the interior through the wall of the container in the area of your service box.

The diagram for the placement of services should be a part of your initial plan. You will want to know where your electric service box will go, arrange the bathroom and kitchen so that they are both near the water and sewage line, and generally have an idea of how you will run the electrics so that all rooms have the necessary power and phone access. When designing your home, clearly mark the services plan over the diagram of your home so that you can build accordingly.

The diagrams below give an indication of how services could be planned for your shipping container home. This is a build which emphasizes efficiency, requiring the least amount of digging and floor removal to accommodate the space:

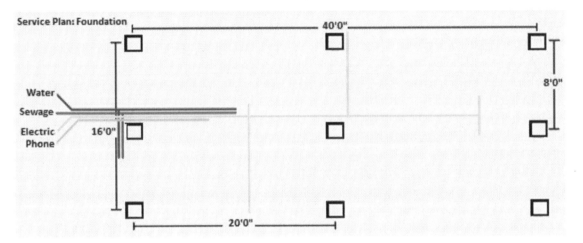

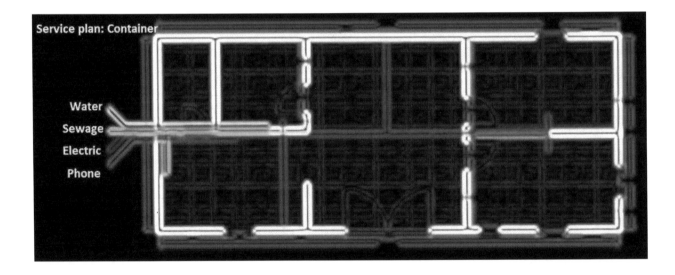

Installing Your Services

Remember that all of the services should be clearly marked on your initial design plan. If you have factored them in from the beginning, the installation should be straightforward, and you will save yourself from costly mistakes later in the process. Here are a few details that will help you to think through the process of services installation.

Electric Services

The first question when arranging electric services is where you plan to install your service panel. The electrics can either be run underground to attach to the service box or run along the roof of the containers. If you choose to weld the containers together, then you will be unable to run the electric line down between the containers, so running it underground will be the only option.

In most areas, building regulations require electrics to be run by a certified electrician. First, find out the building regulations for your area. Electricity can be tricky to play with, so unless you are certain that you have the necessary technical know-how, reach out to a local electrician to make sure the cables are run safely. Another thing to bear in mind is that shipping containers are metal boxes, and that metal conducts electricity very well. Because of this you will want to ground the line, earthing the whole structure with a grounding rod.

Drill through the structure to attach the service securely, and then run the electric line along the centerline of the home. For first fix services, all that is necessary is to run the electric line to the service box, and then through the wall of the container into the interior. Second fix services will then involve installing an interior electric box and running power to all desired locations in the house.

For second fix services, you will want to run lines to every planned light fixture and power outlet, ensuring that all rooms have the desired access to electricity. Run the cables in the areas between the internal studs so that they will be concealed with the interior walls. The route for your power cable should be clearly marked in the design phase, and the actual installation should be left to a certified electrician.

The following diagrams demonstrate one simple plan for running the electricity to a small dwelling and indicate the method of placing the cable in the space between interior studs. This will be covered more fully in Chapter 11, which deals with second fix services.

Electricity layout

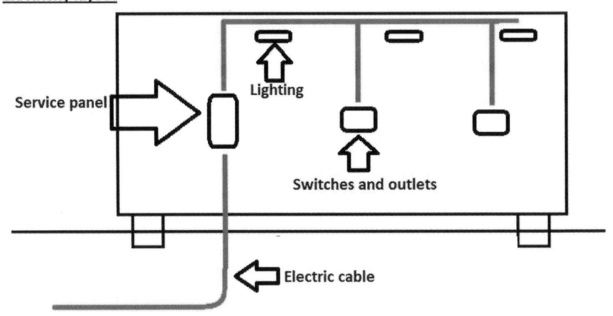

Service panel

Lighting

Switches and outlets

Electric cable

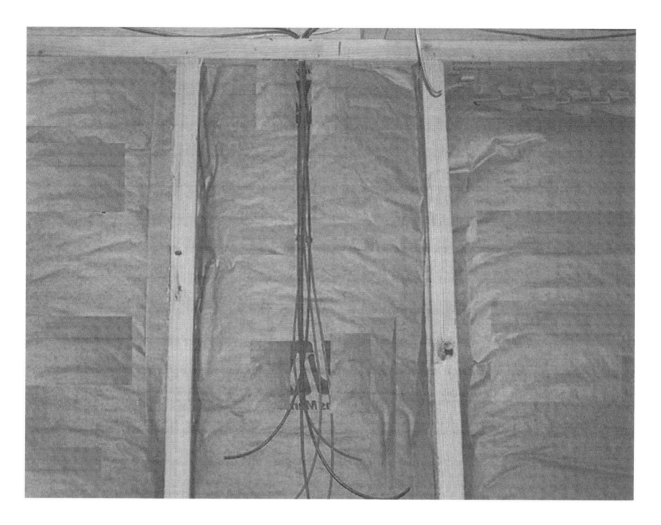

Sewage Installation

The biggest thing that you need to remember about installing your sewage is that it runs on the force of gravity. This means that you need to allow for a drop between the drains and the run of the pipe away from the home. You will need to drill through the bottom of the container to allow space for the pipe to pass through. Run a vertical length of pipe through the drilled hole, and then connect an elbow to direct the flow of sewage toward the outlet. The other end of the line will be run to the sewage outlet. In remote or rural areas, the sewage outlet will be a septic tank, while in urban areas, you will be running your sewage pipes to the main sewer.

Since gravity is the force that drives your sewage, the farther the source of the outlet, the deeper the sewage line will need to be. Also, you will need to ensure that your sewage line is placed below the freeze depth of your area. These are, therefore, the two requirements to be considered when planning the depth of your sewage line.

The rule of thumb is to ensure that the pipe drops ¼ in. per foot of travel. This means that you will need a 1-ft. drop for 48 ft. of travel. The bare minimum of drop is 1/8 in. per foot, though you will have far fewer problems with the previous recommendation. Additionally, this means that a 2-ft. drop from the drain will reach 96 ft., theoretically. However, due to the resistance caused by horizontal travel, you will probably want to expect it to travel only 75 ft.

Another consideration is based completely upon efficiency. To avoid running two sewage lines distant from one another, you will want to try to arrange your plan so that all drains can empty into the same line. This means that you will want to make the kitchen and bathroom close to one another in your plan. This is not always possible, especially with more complicated builds. However, it should be considered a central goal in simpler builds.

Below is a simple diagram demonstrating a sample sewage line for a single container home:

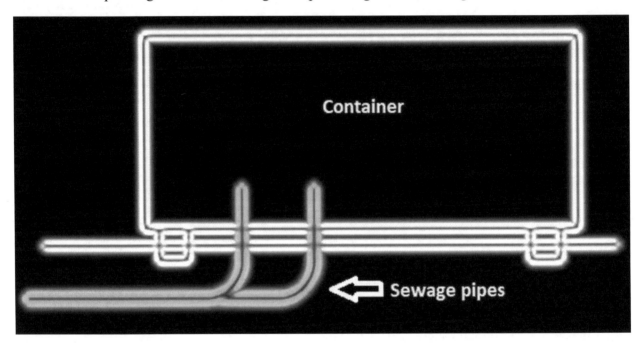

Water Line Installation

The first step in supplying your house with a water line is to dig a trench to house the pipes. The water pipe should be no less than 350mm (14 in.) from electricity and other services. Furthermore, you will want to dig the trench at least 750mm (3.5 ft.) down. If the frost depth for your area is lower than this, then make sure that the run of your pipe is placed beneath frost depth. Your local planning authority will be able to provide you specifics on the frost depth in your area. Ensure that the width of the trench is no less than 300mm (1 ft.), providing plenty of space to lay all necessary pipes.

A few other considerations when running your water pipes: First, they should be filled with sand rather than gravel or rubble. The inlet of your water pipe will need to be run to a water main in urban environments and to a well with a pump in more remote settings. You can use the same trench for the water and sewage pipes, and this will save a bit of digging. However, it is unnecessary to ensure that the pipe has a specific fall per foot, as water pressure provides the force which pushes the water through the line.

Offered below are a few diagrams which show the placement of the water pipes and the combined water/sewage trench:

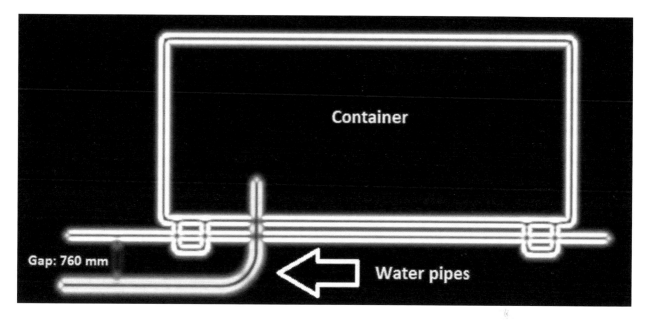

Fitting water and sewage pipes

Sewage and water pipe

Telephone Line Services

Just as the sewage and water lines can be run alongside one another, the phone line and electric line can be wired together. Just as with the electric line, the telephone line can be run either through the roof or the bottom of the container. A third option is to drill directly through the container at the location of the service box and lead both the electric and phone lines through at this entrance point. If you opt for this approach, you will want to seal the entry point well. For raft foundations, you will need to install the phone line through the space of the foundation before laying the concrete of the foundation. Regardless of your foundation, it is visually more appealing to run the line beneath the container.

When burying the phone line, remember to keep the trench at least 350mm (14 in.) away from the water line. The phone line can be run inside a PVC tube with an inner diameter of 22mm. Run the phone line up through the base of the container and then use mastic to seal the holes.

Offered below is a diagram which demonstrates one of the simplest plans for the installation of a telephone line for a single-container dwelling:

First Fix Services Installation Checklist

- Make sure to plan out the services when arranging the initial design.
- Place the service box in the most convenient location for access both inside the container and to the desired areas within the container.
- If possible, plan the drains for the kitchen and bathroom so that they can be close to one another and use a single outlet.
- Arrange the phone line so that it can be laid alongside the electric line.
- Arrange the sewage line so that it can be laid alongside the water line.
- Ensure that the water line is at least 350mm (14 in.) from the electric line.
- Place the horizontal runs of pipe below the frost line.
- When laying the sewage, make sure that you have ¼ in. of drop for each foot of travel.

Chapter 8 – Doors, Windows, and the Removal of Interior Walls

There are two aspects to constructing the interior of your home. The first has been addressed in part in a previous chapter: conversion. Converting your container involves cutting away portions of container walls to create larger adjoining spaces and cutting spaces for doors and windows. To determine the dimensions of the walls which need removal, consult your plan. You can use an angle grinder, plasma torch, or other cutting tool to remove portions of the steel container walls.

The example below shows a design of two adjoining containers, demonstrating where the walls of both containers must be removed.

Electricity layout

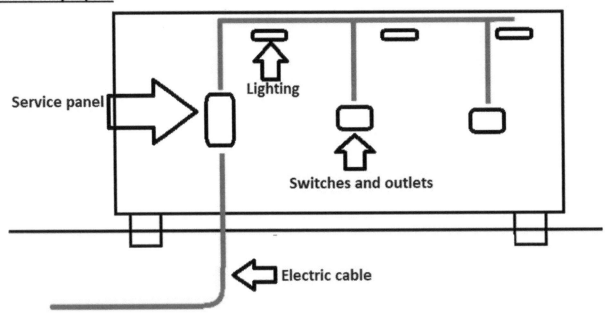

in order to create the larger open space of the front room. Also indicated on the plan are the spaces which must be removed to allow for windows and doors.

Wall layout

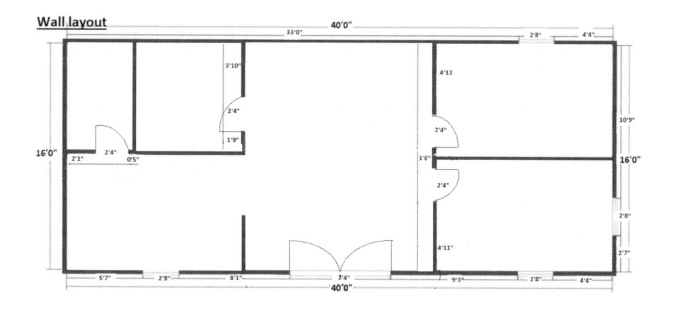

Creating Larger Spaces/Rooms With Adjoining Containers

The first step in converting your containers is to remove the walls of adjacent containers where necessary. This will help to convert two separate containers into a larger connected space. It will not be necessary for designs that utilize only a single container. For these designs, all that is necessary is to frame the interior to partition the interior of the container into different rooms. However, when creating a space composed of the interior of multiple containers, you will want to cut away the walls between them and weld the adjoining floors.

In order to create a larger space, you must first ensure that the containers are seated flush to one another. Spray foam insulation between the two containers and ensure that they are attached firmly to one another through clamping, welding, or bolting. The methods for connecting containers have been discussed above.

If your containers have been converted offsite, you will only need to ensure that the cut-aways of the interior walls line up with one another. If converting onsite, you do not have to be so concerned with this, as you can simply cut through the walls wherever they line up. Consult your plan to determine which walls need removal. If converting offsite, you will need to have clear plans and to mark the containers well before placement, to ensure that each container is placed in the appropriate position to create larger and more complex designs.

Although this has been mentioned above, it is necessary to touch once again upon connecting the floors, roofs, and walls of adjoining containers. Once pre-converted containers have been seated flush, or once walls have been removed between adjoining containers, the floors and roofs must be connected securely. The advised method for this is with welding. A 2 in. x 1/8 in. steel bar can be used to join containers, securely fastened to the steel of both containers with a stitch weld.

The picture below shows the result when joining the floors of two containers in this fashion:

Before cutting away interior walls or archways, mark the cut area and ensure that the measurements meet the desired specifications. Then follow the markings with a cutting disk, plasma torch, angle grinder, or other cutting tool. Have caution during this process, as the slabs of steel from the container walls are heavy and the edges of the steel will be sharp after cutting.

The following pictures show the archway cut between adjoining containers in the example home. Here is a picture of the archway marked out and the cutting process begun:

Cutting out the internal wall from the 2 containers

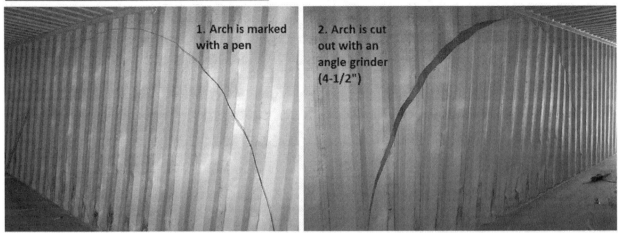

1. Arch is marked with a pen

2. Arch is cut out with an angle grinder (4-1/2")

Remember that once adjoining walls are removed, it will be necessary to weld the floors together so that your structure results in a seamless unit. Another important detail is to weld together the interior seam of the walls. If the roof, floor, and walls of the containers have been securely welded together, this step is not absolutely necessary; however, it will improve the integrity of your home and reduce the potential for pests or leaks.

Another important detail is structural reinforcement. If you are removing large sections of connecting wall, it will be necessary to use steel box beams running the width of the container to bear the load of the roof and ceiling. These should be stitch-welded to the interior roofs of the containers. Consult a structural engineer for the load-bearing requirements of your dwelling to ensure that the structural integrity is sufficient to support the required load.

Below, you can see the picture of the completed archway, cut through two adjacent walls:

Framing and Fitting Doors and Windows

At this point, your home should be taking shape nicely. Once you have placed doors and windows, the shell of your dwelling is complete. The first step in this process is to mark the dimensions of the doors and windows. Next we will create frames for them. After this, we mark and cut the containers to create space for them. The frames can then fit into the frames and welded in place, ensuring that all rough areas are smoothed and that the gaps are filled with sealant. The windows and doors are fit into the frames and hung. Finally, any gaps between window or door and frame are also treated with sealant, ensuring that the shell of your home is watertight.

Making the Frames

Measure out the doors and windows. Once you have the measurements, cut lengths of square 50 x 50mm galvanized steel tubing with a 2mm thickness. Cut the ends at 45-degree angles so that they can be stitch-welded together to construct the frames.

In order to ensure that the measurements are correct, lay the frame against the window or door to make sure it fits. If the fit is correct, remove the door or window and then weld the frame together.

Once it has been welded, you can smooth the assembly using a grinder with a flap-disk. Afterwards, spray the entire frame on both sides with galvanized paint. This will help to prevent corrosion.

Creating the Opening

When cutting the opening for the doors and windows, you will follow much the same process as you have for removing interior walls. First, measure the dimensions of the desired opening and mark them out upon the steel wall of the container. Next, using an angle grinder, plasma cutter, or cutting torch, cut the steel carefully and allow the cut section to drop away.

With regard to the measurement, the easiest method is to use a cardboard cutout sized to the dimensions of your window. Simply place a sheet of cardboard against your window and cut it to the same dimensions. Make sure to include the frame in your template, as the opening will need to be large enough to house it. You can then use this as a template to mark the exterior wall of the container. After marking the wall clearly, cut through the steel with a welding torch, plasma cutter, or angle grinder.

A plasma cutter will offer the cleanest lines and is preferable if you are planning to re-use the steel. However, some may not have access to this tool or the experience to use it properly. If this is the case, then an angle-grinder is the cheapest and most DIY-friendly option. With an angle-grinder, though, it is difficult to cut an accurate and straight line. To do it with ease will require a bit of experience, but if you work slowly and surely, you will be able to make the desired cuts. Once the opening has been cut, you can use a flap disk to smooth out the rough edges.

Hanging Your Doors and Windows

In order to hang your doors and windows, place the frames that you have created inside the openings. Weld the frame into place using a stitch weld. The weld will leave some rough edges, so these can be smoothed out with a flap disk. You can then place the window or frame inside the frame and weld it into place, once more using a stitch weld. Another option is to use self-tapping screws to fix the windows or doors securely in place.

Afterwards, you will want to re-cover any metal that has been bared with galvanized paint, once again to prevent rust. Pay special attention to the corners, as they will have received most attention during this process. If any gaps remain between the frame and container, they can be filled with silicone to prevent leaks. Caulk is ideal for the sides of the windows or doors, and mortar is also an option for filling any remaining gaps between frame and container. Once the gaps have been sealed, you can cover the entire assembly with latex paint to reduce leakage and rust.

The next step can be omitted if you have built a roof with an overhang. However, if not, you will want to make sure to place a rain deflector above any openings you have cut. This can be done simply by welding a 2 in. x 1/8 in. steel plate a few inches above the opening and welding it into place with a stitch weld. This will prevent water from running onto the frame of the door or window and reduce the likelihood of leakage.

The pictures below demonstrate the process of creating both a template and a frame, and show the container in the example home cut to create space for the windows:

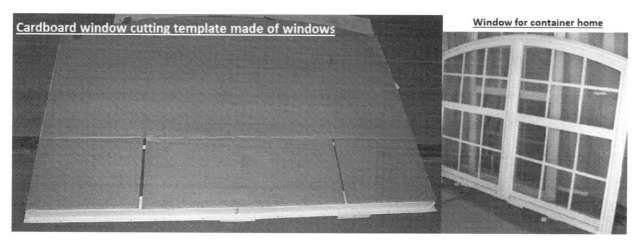

Steel Window Frame

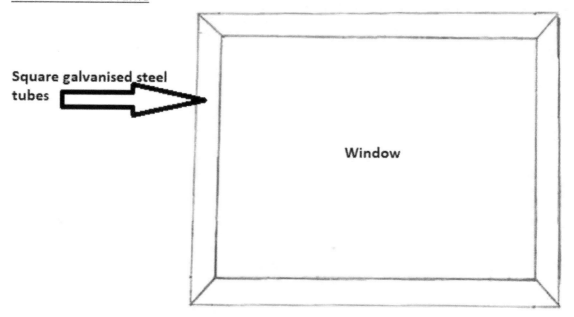

Square galvanised steel tubes

Window

Doors, Windows, and Removal of Interior Walls Checklist

- Measure, mark, and cut away adjoining walls to make larger interior spaces.

- Create the frames for your doors and windows.

- Measure and cut the openings for your doors and windows.

- Weld window frames and doorframes into place.

- Hang windows and doors, securing them in place.

- Smooth the welds, cover with sealant, and cover exposed areas with latex paint.

Chapter 9 – Framing the Interior

You have now established the shell of your home, built the roof, and installed both windows and doors. The house is watertight, and the first fix services have been installed. The next step is to frame the interior of the house.

Once again, you will need to consult the plan to establish where the interior walls need to be placed. The interior walls partition the container into separate rooms. Interior framing is sometimes known as stud-walling. It involves placing a framework of studs to receive plasterboard and paneling for the interior walls.

It is a personal and design choice to frame the external-facing walls of your container. This is not absolutely necessary; however, it will provide battens to house panel or blanket insulation and offer a frame to hang drywall or wall paneling. If you prefer to work instead with the existing walls of the container, then only the partitioning walls require stud wall placement. Remember that if this is your design choice, and if you wish to insulate the interior walls, then you will need to use spray foam insulation for the interior.

Containers can be framed either with wood or steel. Steel will offer you about an inch more of space around the perimeter of each interior wall; however, it is more expensive to work with and requires more specialized tools. Wood is far cheaper and the loss of 1 in. of space around interior walls is usually not much of an issue.

The diagram below shows a plan with the walls which need framing indicated by thick black lines. This design utilizes two 40-ft. containers and will require a portion of the central walls to be cut out in the process of conversion. The interior perimeter of the existing framework must be framed, as well as any partitioning walls which establish the interior rooms.

Setting the Beams

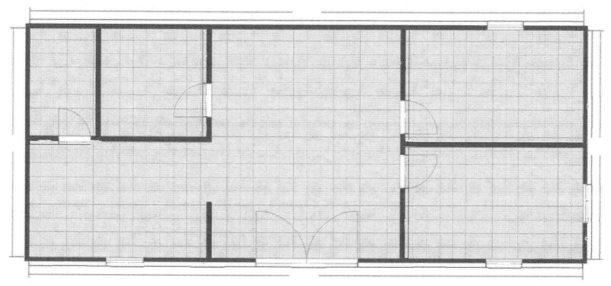

The first step in framing the interior walls is establishing head and sole plates, the beams which line the roof and floor of the container along the line of the interior walls: 2 x 4 in. wooden beams are ideal for this purpose. The head plates can be installed into the roof of the container using $2^{1/2}$ in. self-tapping screws. The sole plates, those which line the floor of the interior walls, can be nailed into place directly into the wooden floor of the container. Use an interval of 2 ft. between screws or nails when affixing the roof and sole plates into the container.

Keep in mind that you will need to ensure that the flooring of the container is either lined with a non-breathable material or replaced with new material. This will ensure that any chemicals in the original flooring are removed or otherwise kept from contaminating the living space. If you opt to place non-breathable material over the exposed flooring, then you will be able to frame the container previous to addressing the flooring. If you choose to replace the flooring with new material, then this step comes before framing the interior.

Placing the Battens

The battens or vertical studs of the walls can then be nailed or screwed firmly into place between the head and sole plates. The first batten should be affixed both to the head and sole plates and the end-wall itself. Each batten thereafter should be measured out so that its center is 40cm (about 16 in.) from the previous: $2^{1/2}$ in. self-tapping screws can be used for this purpose, or, if you are nailing instead of screwing, you can use 50mm nails.

For either option, use a skew pattern, screwing or nailing twice for each batten with each at an angle 25 degrees from the vertical. This will offer the batten a fair amount of resistance to lateral pressure. This pattern should be repeated at both the base and the head of the batten.

One of the best ways to begin this process is to line the interior perimeter of your container. Once you have done that, you can move inward, lining the interior walls of partitioning rooms. This involves providing stud walls for the width of the container and creating the dividing walls that form the shell of each room.

Interior Doors

When making space for interior doors, remember to create space between the battens or studs and place a noggin, or horizontal beam, above the space for the door. This creates an upper beam above the door to which you can later affix plasterboard. If you have gone to great lengths in planning the interior layout of your home, you will also know where you plan to hang heavy items like mirrors and other hefty wall-hanging articles. If you do know, then place a noggin, or horizontal beam, between studs, to offer a secure place for fixing these items later on.

After the stud-walling has been completed, you will then be in a place to hang your internal doors. If they have been bought re-framed, you may need to shim them level after placing them into the opening. Once you have ensured that it is level, simply nail it into place. If you are framing the doors yourself, follow the same method to ensure that the frame is level before affixing the structure to the battens.

Tips: If you happen to be using thicker plasterboard, then you will want the studs placed closer together. Use a spacing of 30cm or 1 ft. instead of the 40cm suggested for lighter plasterboard. Also ensure that you have placed battens wherever plasterboard sheets will meet, especially above doors or windows.

Another key involves ceiling installation. If you would like to install a ceiling, then you can affix joists to the roof of the container with 2 ½ in. self-tapping screws and attach the head plates beneath the roof joists. This will leave a gap between the head plates and the roof of the container.

Framing the Interior – Checklist

- Decide whether you would like to install a ceiling. If so, attach roof joists prior to framing the interior.
- Use self-tapping screws to attach the head and sole plates of the stud walls.
- Line the head and sole plates with battens, leaving space for doors and openings.
- Place noggins between studs over interior doors and openings. Also place noggins where you know that you will hang heavy objects from the walls.
- Hang interior doors.

Chapter 10 – Ceiling Installation

Ceiling installation, as with many things in the construction of your shipping container home, is a personal choice. An exposed roof has its own aesthetic appeal. It gives a clear indication of the container before the home. This comes down to a personal preference.

Exposed Ceilings

Leaving the ceilings exposed is the cheapest option and the fastest build. At the same time, this reduces the amount of insulation with which you can line your home, and an exposed ceiling tends to collect condensation from cooking. So, opting to leave the original roof bared both sets you up for higher heating and cooling costs and creates potential problems in the form of rust and mold.

Therefore, it is recommended to install a ceiling in your home. This is doubly important if you have chosen not to install an additional roof. Without either an additional roof or ceiling, you have very little in the way of insulation for the roof of your container, and this is one of the most crucial locations where heat loss can be prevented.

Ceiling Installation

The first step in ceiling installation is to install roof joists. You have a couple of options here. You can either screw the joists directly into the roof of the container with 2 ½ in. self-tapping screws or nail them to the head plates of the stud walls. You will save a couple of inches of space by attaching joists to the upper roof beams of the steel container; however, you will need to do this before framing your container. Also, if choosing this option, you may either choose to cut the plasterboard ceilings around the head plate of the wall battens or install the full ceiling and then affix the head plates to the joists after the entire ceiling has been installed.

Position the joists so that the centers of the joists are 400mm apart from one another. Once the joists have been placed, if you choose to insulate the ceiling, install insulation between the joists. Next, place either paneling or drywall over the joists and screw them into place.

Another option is to use a suspended ceiling; however, this doesn't make much sense in a shipping container home, as space is at a premium. The maximum height is 8 ft.10 in., the space you will have with a high cube container, so you may want to consider how to accomplish your needs with the least necessary width. The only advantage of suspended ceilings is that you will have space above them to run utility cables and pipes and to place additional insulation.

Tips: Even if choosing not to place insulation, you will want to place plastic sheeting as a vapor barrier. Also, you will want to remember that shipping containers are often painted with materials that contain dangerous chemicals, such as phosphorus. Check with the container manufacturer to find out what chemicals have been used for the container, and if any hazardous chemicals have been used, look into the sealants that can be used to prevent the release of toxic fumes.

Ceiling Installation – Checklist
- Decide whether to install a ceiling or leave it bare.
- Secure roof joists to the head plates or to the roof of the container.
- Place insulation between the roof joists.
- Cover the joists with panels or drywall sheets and screw them into place.

Chapter 11 – Second Fix Services

For second fix services, you will want to run the utilities from the point where they enter the container to the points where water, electric, telephone, and drainage will serve the needs of the home. This involves fitting electric sockets, light switches, lighting, phone lines, plumbing, and any other utility services to the desired location on the interior of your home.

The first step in this process, your first fix services, will make sure that you have access to the basic services needed for all of your utilities. Water has been run from either the pump or the city water main, sewage has been linked from either the septic tank or sewer to the main drains of your home. Electrics have been run to the service box and into the interior of the container. Second fix services involve running the utility lines from the entry point to the points of service.

Electric Services

The electric lines can be run in a number of ways. You can either drill a hole in the ceiling and run the wire through the area above the ceiling or line the surface of the ceiling with the lines. The first option is more aesthetically pleasing. The second is easier, and will be DIY simple. If you choose to run the cable above the ceiling, you may choose to do this after attaching the joists but before attaching the ceiling panels.

The first step in wiring the second-service electrics is to run the main electric line into the container and wire this into the service panel. From the service panel, you can then lead the electrics up to the ceiling and then through the container across the length of the container to the light switches, outlets, and light fixtures.

Romex wire is a flexible, non-metallic cable which is ideal for this purpose. The Romex wire can be sheathed in a plastic self-adhesive trunking, a plastic tubing designed to protect cables. This trunking can then be run to the desired location, affixed to the battens along the length of the run and held in position with staples, tape wiring, or plastic clips.

If you choose not to use trunking, then you can fix the wires into place with tape wire, leading them through the battens as indicated below.

The diagrams below offer a couple of examples for wiring the second-service electrics through the interior of your home. The blue lines indicate how the electrics might be run through the interior of your home to provide for outlets, light fixtures, and light switches:

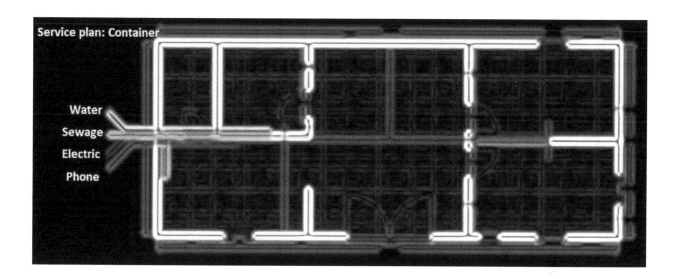

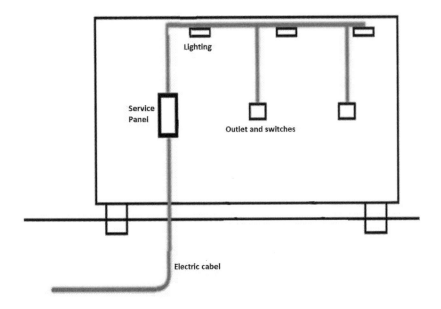

After placing the run of the electric lines, the next step is to attach the electric outlets, light fixtures, and light switches and to wire the electric lines into them. These should be affixed to the battens and roof joists to make them secure.

Remember: Electric work is dangerous and requires the skills and knowledge of a skilled technician. Employ the services of a skilled technician to ensure that the electrics are installed properly.

Water and Sewage

Once the first fix services have been installed, you will have both water and sewage lines run to the interior of the container. Vertical pipes for each will have been run up through the floor of the container. As mentioned in the chapter above on first fix services, portions of the floor will have been removed to accommodate this installation. Observe the image below to have an idea of how this will look in the building process.

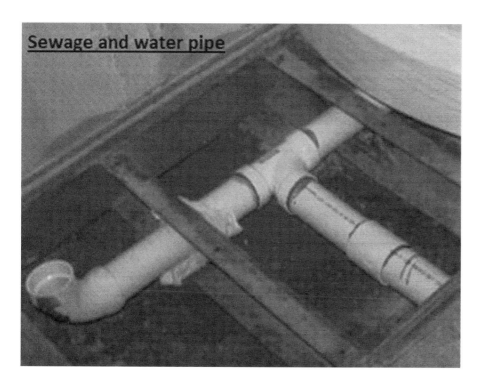

Sewage and water pipe

The pipes must now be prepared for all sinks, showers, and toilets. Run the plumbing so that all drains lead to the sewage drain, and all water pipes to the water main. Install a stop tap to make sure that you can cease the flow of water in the event of a plumbing issue. You'll thank yourself for this when a leak occurs.

Water and sewage are pretty straightforward in regard to second-fix services. You simply need to run all the drains to the main sewage output, and run all the faucets to the water main. If you have designed your home so that these are close together, you can use a minimum of pipe to make this happen.

Telephone Services

Once the first fix services have been completed, the telephone line will have been run to the interior of the container sheathed in PVC and buried beneath the ground until it has been raised into the container. One option is to run the electric line through the service box of the electrics, and another is to drill a hole in the floor of the container and run the line upwards into the container at the location where the telephone jack unit will be placed.

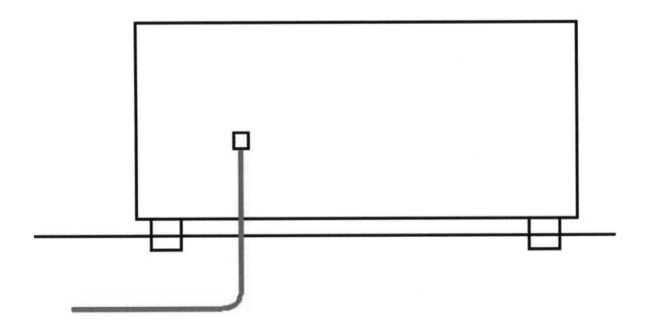

For the lift of the line, run it against an interior corrugation if possible and tape the loose cable to the corrugated steel. Once the line has been led to the appropriate height, affix the telephone line jack unit into the wooden battens and wire the phone line into it.

The diagram below offers an example of how the phone lines might be run into the interior of the container:

Second Fix Services – Checklist

- Install light fixtures, light switches, and electrical outlets. Run electric lines from the service box to each.
- Attach the drains for showers and sinks to the main sewage outlet.
- Install plumbing to bring water from the main to all sinks and showerheads.
- Install the telephone jack and run the telephone line to it.
- Remember to get professional assistance for electrical installation.

Chapter 12 – Insulation

The issue of insulation is quite an important one. Technically, insulation is not actually required. Also, any steps you can skip during the build process will make the home faster and cheaper to build. However, remember that a shipping container is essentially a large steel box. Steel is an excellent conductor of both heat and cold. So, without proper insulation, you are likely to be freezing in the winter and living in an oven in the summer. You can tough it out in discomfort, or pay extravagant heating or cooling bills.

Another consideration is that without insulation, condensation will tend to collect on the interior walls of the home. Water collecting on the walls can lead to a number of problems down the line, including mold and rust. Mold is a health hazard for you and your family, and corrosion, if left unattended, can eventually cause leaks and damage the integrity of the container. So, while opting to go without insulation might save a few bucks during the initial build, the cost of going without can be much higher than the cost of installing it.

Insulation Options

If you do opt for insulation, then you have a number of choices. One of the first choices is whether to insulate the exterior of the container or the interior. Exterior insulation is preferable for cold climates, as it will reduce the loss of heat from the container itself into the colder air around it. You can also use a combination of internal and external insulation or use both. If you are building in an extreme climate, then doubling up may be the best choice.

External Insulation

There are a number of advantages to external insulation. First, as mentioned above, it is more effective in reducing both heating and cooling of the container itself. As a result, external insulation is more effective than internal in reducing heating and cooling costs and maintaining a comfortable interior temperature.

External insulation can also be helpful for aesthetic purposes. Spray foam insulation can smoothen the surface of your container, readying it to receive a layer of paint or cladding. This will be explored more fully in Chapter 16, which addresses your options for finishing the exterior of your home.

A final advantage is that external insulation will preserve the interior height and width of the container. Since you are working with a limited height, this is an important consideration. External insulation of the floor of the container makes both the installation of a subfloor and the placement of insulation beneath this subfloor unnecessary. In addition, it will prevent both corrosion and pests. Even if you choose to use interior insulation for every other part of your home, external insulation is the best option for the floor of the container.

If you had planned to leave the interior walls of the container unmodified, then external insulation is ideal as it will let you preserve every available inch of floor space. Similarly, if your design involves leaving the original ceiling of the container as is, then adding insulation can result in a loss of valuable height. The situation is a bit different if you are planning to install a ceiling, and/or add paneling or drywall to the interior studs. In this case, you lose no additional space by insulating the space between the roof beams or wall studs.

Internal Insulation

As mentioned above, internal insulation is an excellent option if you plan to panel the walls and install a ceiling. In these instances, you lose no additional floor space or height. Although internal insulation of the ceiling will result in a loss of height, it is still recommended, as it will prevent the buildup of condensation on the roof of the container when cooking.

If you are building with a used container, then it may have scratches, dents, or marks on the inner walls. Internal insulation can cover a marred surface and provide a surface to paint on. Furthermore, you then have the option of leaving the exterior of the container as is. Though not recommended in colder climates, this does offer a certain aesthetic appeal.

The most important thing to keep in mind with regard to internal insulation is the space that it takes up. Since you are working with limited space to begin with, you'll want to preserve as much as possible. However, this is only a limiting factor in certain circumstances, as indicated above. You will also have the option of insulating internally for some areas and externally for others, or doubling up and insulating both externally and internally.

Placement of Insulation

Essentially, you will want to insulate all six faces of the container. This means all external-facing walls, the roof, and the floor. For each of these placements, either external or internal insulation is an option. If you have added a roof on the container, then you will be able to place insulation in the space between the roof of the container and the roof you have built. It will be important to keep this in mind when building the roof, as you will not have the option once the roof has been built.

If you have chosen to frame the interior walls, then insulation can be placed between the studs. Similarly, when installing a ceiling, you will have the option of insulating between the roof beams. If you have chosen to skip external insulation of the floor of the container, then it would be best to insulate the inner floor and install a subfloor.

The figures below show the placement of insulation between the battens of the interior wall and indicate the cavity of the roof which can be used for insulation:

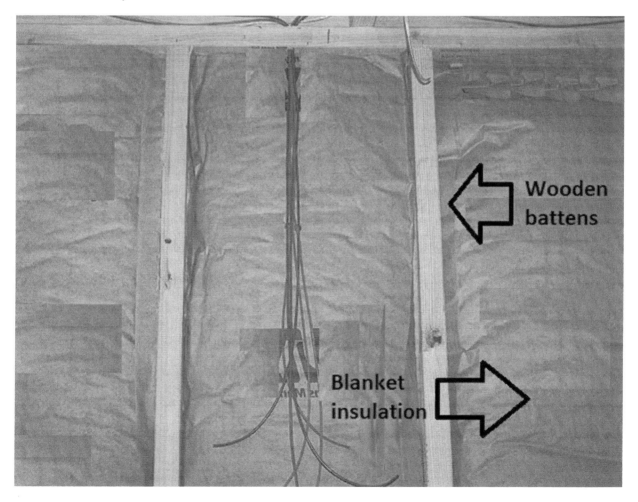

Insulation roof

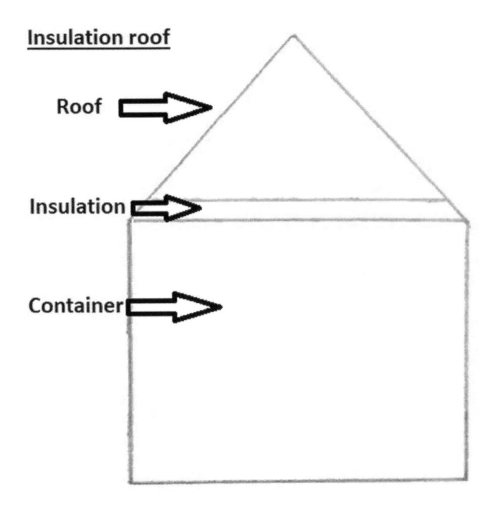

Roof

Insulation

Container

Types of Insulation

There are a few types of installation available to you, and each has certain advantages and disadvantages. The options are: spray foam, insulation panels, and blankets or rolls. We'll explore each of them in the following sections.

Blanket Insulation

Blanket insulation is the cheapest of the three options. The most common style of blanket insulation is mineral, and it is commonly known as "rock wool."

Installation requires the construction of stud walls, as the rock wool rolls are placed between the battens. Once the stud walls have been constructed, it is quick and easy to place. The installation is simple, but it should be remembered that blanket insulation is made of fiberglass and should be handled carefully.

If you choose not to use spray foam to insulate the underside of the container, then rock wool is a relatively simple and cheap alternative. If you choose to combine methods, you can place rock wool and then spray an inch of spray foam over it. This will increase the insulating qualities of the layer and provide an airtight seal. One thing to remember is that you will need to batten out the foundation in order to place the blanket insulation between the battens.

Tip: Some types of blanket insulation use formaldehyde as a binder. To reduce the hazardous chemicals in your home, look for formaldehyde-free blanket insulation. This has the same insulating properties without the harsh chemicals.

Panel Insulation

Panel insulation is slightly more expensive than blanket insulation, but it is the easiest of all the methods to install. It also goes up quicker than blanket insulation. Furthermore, it is easier to handle, as you won't have to worry about fiberglass particles, and you won't have to tape everything up to prevent mess.

Panel insulation is just what it sounds like. It is a relatively thin panel with a high insulating value. These panels can be bought in predefined sizes and placed between studs, so the installation process is almost exactly like that of blanket insulation; however, they are thinner and will leave you more space to work with. Unless you're going for the absolute cheapest option, ease of installation and reduced thickness make panel insulation worth the few extra bucks.

Panel insulation can also be used for the underside of the container, though, just as with blanket insulation, the foundation will need to be battened out to affix the panels.

Spray Foam Insulation

Spray foam insulation is the most expensive option and requires a bit more skill to install. It is also quite messy, so you will need to cover everything that you don't want covered by spray foam prior to application. However, it is the quickest method and offers the most effective insulation.

Spray foam creates a seamless airtight barrier and provides the highest resistance to heat flow for a given thickness. In layman's terms, it insulates best. Another advantage that it has over blanket and panel insulation is that it can easily fill uneven surfaces and gaps, whereas blanket and panel insulation might have to be cut down to fill odd spaces.

There are a number of options on the market when it comes to spray foam. What you're looking for is closed-cell polyurethane foam. Closed-cell spray foam is resistant to both water and vapor.

It can be used externally or internally, while open-cell spray foam should only be used internally in areas which will not be subject to dampness. Closed-cell polyurethane foam also has a higher insulating value per applied thickness. When space is a premium, every inch counts.

Remember: Regardless of the type of insulation you choose, remember to use the proper PPE, or personal protective equipment. This includes dust masks, goggles, gloves, and protective clothing.

Installation

Blanket or Panel Insulation

When compared to spray foam, installing blanket or panel insulation is far cleaner, but it takes a bit more time and effort. You will need to have a stud wall framed prior to installation. After the wall has been framed, the same steps are followed for both blankets and panels.

Essentially, all that is required is to place the panels or blankets in the gaps between the studs. Try to plan the placement of your battens and the width of your blankets or panels so that they can be placed in the gaps without cutting. This will increase the ease of installation and reduce the build time. For blanket insulation, place the foil side of the insulation against the wall of the container.

If you choose to use blanket or panel installation on the exterior floor or the roof of your container, then you will need to ensure that these areas are battened out beforehand. For the roof of the container, simply affix 2 x 4 in. battens across the beams used for the roof trusses. Space them so that the centers of the battens are separated by 400mm. The process of battening out the foundation is similar, but you will first need to attach beams across the length of the foundation to hold the battens.

Spray Foam Insulation

As mentioned above, spray foam is messy. It goes on quick and is extremely effective as an insulation material, as well as being the best for fitting into small gaps and odd spaces. Spray foam insulation can also be sprayed directly onto the walls of the container, meaning that you will save time in creating battens if they aren't necessary for other purposes (like holding up paneling for interior walls).

The first step in placing spray foam insulation is covering anything that you *don't* want covered with spray foam. This includes doors and windows, as well as pipes, utility cables, and electric sockets. A thin layer of plastic sheeting will do the trick. Cut it to size, and then fit in place with masking tape. Cables, pipes, and electric sockets can be wrapped in tape before beginning the process. You may also want to place a plastic sheet on the floor of the container, to prevent overspray and time-consuming cleanup later.

Though it isn't necessary to frame the inner surface of exterior walls if insulating with spray foam, you may still choose to do so. This will allow you to place plasterboard or paneling over the insulation. Plasterboard will offer a smooth surface which can then be painted, while panels offer their own unique aesthetic value. If you have chosen to go this route, simply spray foam insulation between the battens, just as you would have placed blankets or panels.

If you choose not to frame the external-facing walls, then you may choose to use different nozzles when applying the spray foam. This will offer a variety of textures to the wall, ranging from smooth to pebbled.

With spray foam insulation, you will need a minimum of 2 in. of foam thickness on the walls. You have some options here. You can spray the entire 2 in. on one side of the wall, either the interior or the exterior, or you can instead divide it, placing 1 in. on the inside and 1 in. on the outside.

If your design involves joining two or more containers together, make sure to insulate the bolts joining the walls and the welds between adjoining floors. Place a layer of spray foam over the flat metal bars which were welded between adjoining walls, as well as over and around the bolts placed between containers.

Tip: Before beginning placement, spray the foam inside an empty box. This will clear propellant from the nozzle and give you an idea of the rate at which the foam comes out of the nozzle. Once you have gauged the rate, you will be able to apply the insulation with much greater control and fluidity.

Insulation – Checklist

- Choose whether or not you would like to insulate your home, keeping climate in mind.
- If you choose to insulate, select interior or exterior insulation, both, or a combination of the two.
- Select the type of insulation you would like to use. Remember that certain types of insulation are more suitable for certain areas.
- If insulating the bottom of the container, remember to do so before placing it.
- If insulating the roof, remember to do so when constructing it.
- Remember that different types of insulation can be used on the same face of the container.
- When considering insulation, remember that all six faces of the container will need to be addressed.

Chapter 13 – Hanging Drywall and Preparing it for Paint

When it has come time to fit the walls, both the interior and exterior of the container will have been laid out. Your home will be taking shape and almost finished by this point. In this step, you will line the battens with either plasterboard or wall paneling.

If you can get some help in placing the drywall, the process will go much more quickly. You can do it alone; however, this will take a great deal more time and effort.

Fitting Plasterboard or Paneling

When covering the battens with drywall or paneling, begin at the openings such as doors or windows. Move outward from the openings to the farthest walls. Stagger the panels or drywall horizontally, ensuring that the seams do not end up on the same batten. Having a number of seams on the same batten will invite cracks to form down the line.

One key for placing drywall is to set the edges so that they line up with the centers of the battens. Around openings, this may be a challenge; however, it will be possible at all other points along the wall. Screw through plasterboard along the battens, noggins, head plates, and sole plates, ensuring that screws are placed every 200mm or 8 in. Work vertically and horizontally to make sure that each board is attached, one after another.

Tips: Use screws designed specifically for plasterboard. They will be coated with phosphate and have a countersunk head. Also, when you need to cut a board to fit an odd space, first measure it with a tape measure. Next, mark the cut with a spirit level. Then, use a Stanley knife to cut the board. Finally, attach the plasterboard, ensuring that the factory edges of the boards line up with one another.

Preparing Your Plasterboard for Paint

Once the plasterboard has been placed, the next step of the process is to paint it to provide a smooth and appealing finish. With older plasterboards, this would require plaster to be placed over the drywall boards. Plaster provides a layer of protection, evens the surface, and makes redecoration easier.

Newer drywall is designed so that it can be painted over without plaster. If you are painting directly over drywall, you will first need to fill the screw holes and the gaps between drywall sheets. Screw holes can be filled with a jointing compound. You will need to use a small filling knife to pack the joint compound into the screw holes. For the spaces between drywall panels, joint tape can be lined along the edges of the panels. The plasterboard can then be covered with a drywall sealer.

After sealing your walls, you are then ready to paint the drywall. You can follow the instructions in Chapter 15 to find more details in the painting of your interior walls.

Hanging Drywall and Preparing it for Paint – Checklist

- Decide whether you will use drywall or cover your stud walls with other means. Chapter 15 on finishing interior walls will offer a range of other options.
- When hanging drywall, obtain help if possible. An extra pair of hands will make the process go much more quickly and smoothly.
- Use drywall screws. They will have phosphate coatings and countersunk heads.
- Begin hanging from openings and work your way to the opposite wall.
- Set the edges of the drywall in the center of the battens if possible. This should be feasible everywhere except around the openings.
- Stagger the edges of the drywall so that the joints don't line up. This will prevent cracks from forming later.
- Use joint compound to fill the screw holes. Use joint tape and joint compound to fill the gaps between drywall sheets.
- You may want to cover your drywall with drywall sealer. This is not absolutely necessary if you are using a newer drywall, but it is recommended.

Chapter 14 – Flooring

Once you have come to the point of installing your flooring, you are just around the corner from having a fully functional home, ready to move in and begin enjoying as a living space. There are two major steps to this process: dealing with the original flooring and laying the finished flooring.

Subfloor

Most containers come ready with marine plywood. It's quite tempting to simply use this as the flooring of your home, and in some cases, this may be possible. However, for most containers, this flooring will be treated with pesticides and other hazardous chemicals. This makes them unsuitable for use as a flooring as is.

One option, if you are buying new containers, is to confer with the manufacturer to arrange for the flooring to remain untreated. With used and one-time use containers, you will need to either remove or cover the flooring. Either method will ensure that you and your family remain safe from pesticides and other chemicals. The flooring can be covered with either a subfloor or a non-breathable underlay. Finally, a concrete floor can be poured on the original flooring. This leaves us with four flooring options.

Removing Hazardous Flooring

The most direct option is to simply remove the existing flooring of the containers and replace it with new plywood. This is a relatively simple process; however, it can be somewhat time consuming, especially if you are working with multiple containers. The additional plywood costs will also need to be factored into the initial budget.

If there are holes or other damage in the plywood, then removing and replacing the floor may be the only option. If you would like to avoid this step, it will be helpful to examine the floors of the containers before purchase.

It should be remembered that this step will need to be done prior to any interior work on the container, such as installing stud walls and framing the interior.

Installing a Subfloor

If you would like to avoid removal of the original flooring, you may opt to lay a subfloor. The first step in this process is to create a barrier over the existing flooring to prevent chemicals from seeping through the flooring in vapor form.

Begin by cleaning the existing flooring with isopropyl alcohol. Next, coat the floor with a low v epoxy. Low viscosity epoxy works well in damp or high moisture conditions. It is sold in 1.5 gal kits, and each will cover 150-175 sq. ft. One to two coats will seal the floor effectively. This creates a vapor-proof barrier which effectively contains hazardous chemicals.

Next you can cover the epoxy layer with ¾ in. marine plywood. Tongue and groove plywood sheets are ideal for this. To affix the new flooring, 2-in. coated deck screws can be driven directly through the upper layer and into the original flooring.

Optionally, a ¹/² in. layer of foam can be laid over the epoxy barrier before placing the new plywood. This will provide additional insulation. It should be remembered, however, that the installation of a subfloor will cost an inch of height. This option is also as costly as removing the existing flooring and replacing it with new.

Non-Breathable Flooring Underlay

The final option for addressing the flooring is to place an underlay. This is by far the cheapest option. In addition, this can be done after framing the interior, directly prior to installing the finished flooring. It is also quick to lay, requiring the least installation time of any method.

The first step in installing an underlay is identical to that for installing a subfloor. The original flooring should be cleaned and then coated with low v epoxy. Next, cut the underlayment to size and shape. Place over the original flooring and then nail into place through the underlay.

The diagram below shows the placement of the underlay and the flooring after the underlay has been covered with laminate flooring.

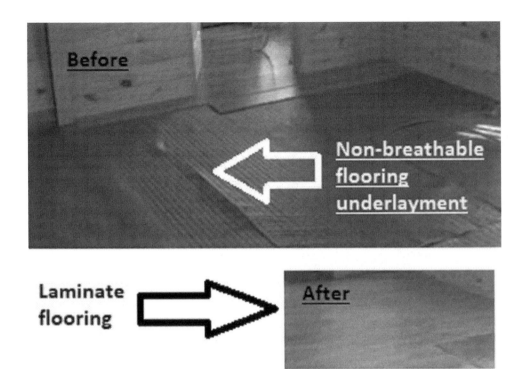

Concrete Flooring

There are many advantages to using a concrete floor, though it has some disadvantages as well. The concrete can be poured directly on the original marine plywood. Once it has been placed and finished, it can be used as a finished flooring. It is quite durable and easy to clean, and it can be dyed, polished, or embellished with a pattern for aesthetic purposes.

As far as the downsides go, concrete tends to collect the cold, so it may not be ideal in colder climates. It will make it more difficult to keep the home heated and may be uncomfortable to walk on. Also, previous to pouring the concrete, 2mm thick steel bars will first need to be welded across the length and width of the room. The bars should be welded one inch above the floor and spaced one foot apart from one another.

After the steel bars have been welded in place, the final step is to pour and finish the concrete. The final downside is that you will need to allow the concrete to cure before continuing work on the interior.

Finishing the Flooring

There are a number of options for the new floor. Concrete, tile, laminate, or carpet can be used. If you choose to opt for concrete, then the subflooring and flooring are completed in a single shot. Concrete, tile, and laminate are ideal in warmer climates, as they will help to keep the house cool.

Cooler climates will benefit from the use of carpet. The following sections will explore the placement of carpet, tile, and laminate.

The first step in laying any flooring is to measure out the floor. You'll need the total square footage of the floor space to know how much carpet, how many tiles, or how many pieces of laminate you will need. You will also need to know the dimensions of each room so that the carpet can be cut to the proper dimensions and so that the tiles or laminate can be divided accordingly.

Laying Carpet

Carpet is more challenging to clean than tile, concrete, or laminate; however, it is more comfortable on the feet, and helps to keep the home warm. It's also a bit easier to install.

The first step in laying carpet is to line the walls of the space with carpet gripper. Essentially, carpet gripper is thin strips of wood with sharp pins protruding from one side. These pins will be used to fix the carpet into place. Carpet gripper should line all of the interior walls of the home for areas where carpet is to be placed.

It's important to leave a gap of 10mm between the wall and the wall-edge of the carpet gripper. Tinsnips can be used to cut the carpet gripper to size. It can then be either nailed down or fixed into place with carpet gripper adhesive.

The next step is to place your carpet underlay. This is a rubber-and-foam layer which provides cushion beneath the carpet. It should be fitted inside the carpet grippers. Placing the rubber side down of the underlay, fit one edge against the carpet gripper against one wall, and then roll out until you reach the opposite wall. Use a utility knife to cut the underlay snug against the carpet gripper of this wall. Repeat this process until you have covered the entire space with underlay, and use carpet tape to seal the joints.

The final step is to lay the carpet in place. First, cut the carpet to the dimensions of the room. Then, lay it out loosely in the room, ensuring that one corner is in position. Move to each other corner, positioning each squarely. Leave an extra 50mm at each edge, as the carpet will stretch somewhat when fit on the grippers.

When fitting your carpet, it's important to begin on the wall opposite the doorway. Fit the carpet down onto the grippers, ensuring that it lays flat. Work backwards towards the door and cut away any excess material with a utility knife.

Laying Floor Tiles

Tile is easy to clean and can be quite beautiful. It is ideal for warmer climates, as it will help to keep the house cool. It is fairly simple to lay tile in a shipping container home, as the spaces for most simple designs will be rectangular. If you have chosen to frame the external facing walls prior to laying tile, then you have also simplified the process of laying tile quite a bit. If not, then you will need to be able to cut the tiles precisely in order to fill the space for the corrugated walls.

There are a number of ways you can lay tile, depending upon the shape of the room and the design of the tile. One of the simplest is to determine the center of the room with chalk lines and work outward from there. This will ensure that the center has a nice look, but will require you to cut the tiles which edge up against the walls.

Another option is to lay the tiles out along one wall and then work, one row at a time, to the opposite wall. If you are laying color patterns in your tile, you may wish to begin from the center of the pattern. You may want to explore a few dry layouts to decide which looks best in the space you are tiling.

Once you have decided your starting point, spread either thinset mortar or floor tile adhesive, keying it in with the flat side of a notched trowel, and then using the notched side to line it into grooves. Both thinset and adhesive will dry quickly, so only cover a small area before laying tile down. Lay the first tile in place and press firmly, then place tile spacers on the corners. Continue laying tiles, fitting each into the previous spacers.

Use a spirit level from time to time to make sure that the tiles are level with one another. Work up to the edges of the room, leaving the odd spaces against the wall for last. This will allow you to measure and cut all the partial tiles in a single run. You will want to back butter the partial tiles and fit them into the spaces that remain.

If using thinset, allow it to cure for 24 hours. Avoid placing your weight upon the newly laid tiles until the thinset cures. The cure time for ceramic tile adhesive is considerably shorter, and will be indicated by the manufacturer. After the thinset or adhesive has been cured, remove the spacers and fill the spaces with grout. Cover small spaces with grout at a time, and then rinse the surface of the tile clean. Cover the grooves with grout sealant.

Tips for professional-looking tile: It is not recommended to tile directly onto plywood. While it is possible, it may result in uneven tiles, and the adhesive or thinset may not adhere well. Instead, you can place a layer of concrete board over the plywood. The concrete board will provide a smooth surface to keep the tiles even.

Lay the concrete board down so that the joints between the boards alternate. Screw the concrete board into the plywood flooring, countersinking the screw heads flush with the surface of the concrete board. Tape and mud the joints between concrete boards. This can then be used as a surface to lay tile.

Another key consideration is whether to use thinset mortar or ceramic tile adhesive. Tile adhesive is easier to work with; however, there are a few drawbacks. First, it is only lightly water resistant. In the event of high-water conditions, adhesive will begin to mold and lose adhesive properties. Adhesive is also not recommended for high-traffic conditions.

Thinset mortar is preferable for floors, as you will be able to fill voids and ensure that the tiles are level. It is also more water resistant and will result in a more durable tile floor. Tile cement is preferable for vinyl and linoleum tiles, while thinset mortar is best for ceramic and porcelain tile.

If using an alternating color pattern, arrange the boxes beforehand so that you know which to pull from when laying. This is especially important if you wish to arrange the tiles in a pattern. This can be tricky, so if you are laying tile for the first time, it may be best to use a simple layout.

Lay down only as much mortar or adhesive as you can work with in ten minutes, and then lay down more once you have covered this and added spacers.

Laying Laminate Flooring

Laminate flooring can either be laid upon a subfloor or on a non-breathable underlay directly over the original plywood. If you choose to lay the flooring prior to framing the container, then you can begin working from the left-hand corner of each container. If you have framed the container first, then you can begin at the left-hand corner opposite the door of each room.

Once you have laid the first board, place the next end-on to the previous. Slide the board down at a 30-degree angle, and then lower the other end into place, snugging the ends together as you bring it flat and lock it into place. Continue placing boards until you have completed the first row, cutting the final piece to length if necessary. This can be done easily by laying the final piece over the previous and then marking the desired length. Cut along the marking and then insert the final board in the remaining space.

One key to placing a durable laminate floor is to stager the joints. You will want to cut a new board in half to begin the next row of laminate. Place the cut edge against the wall, and then slide it forward to lock it into the previous row. The final row of boards may need to be cut to size. The length can be measured just as the end-board is measured, by laying the piece length-wise over the previous row and marking the width that remains.

Laying laminate will be far easier if you frame the container previous to placing laminate. Otherwise, you will need to trim the laminate boards around the corrugated walls of the container. This is time consuming and delicate and missed cuts may result in the waste of materials.

Observe the image below to see how laminate boards lock together:

Flooring – Checklist

- If you are ordering a new container, request that it be constructed with the floors untreated with chemicals.
- Either remove the original flooring or fix any damaged areas.
- Decide on your subflooring. Either remove old plywood and replace new, cover the existing plywood with a non-breathable underlay, use a non-breathable underlay and add a subfloor, or lay concrete flooring.
- Decide on the finished flooring. Options include tile, laminate, carpet, or concrete. Keep the climate in mind. Carpet is better for colder climates, while tile, laminate, and concrete are better in warmer climates.
- Remember that a concrete board subfloor is recommended if laying tile.

Chapter 15 – Finishing Interior Walls

Walls, floor, and ceiling. This is the shell of the house, the elements that form the fundamental feel of your new home. And, just like for every other aspect of home construction, you have some options. The most traditional option is to simply hang drywall and apply some paint. You can dress up the drywall with plaster if you would like to apply a veneer plaster wall. A veneer of thin wood can be placed over the drywall as well. Another option is to use textured wall panels.

If you would like to avoid drywall altogether, you can opt for real wood paneling or even plywood. There are also a number of pre-made wall panels which could be used, such as wahoo walls or basement wall finishing systems. Another option, more time consuming, but quite durable and aesthetically pleasing, is to use a plaster and lath system. This involves placing hundreds of horizontal wood slats and plastering over them.

In this section, we will explore only two of these methods: real wood and painted drywall. However, the remainder of the techniques will be self-explanatory once you understand the principles behind these two.

Painted Drywall

Drywall is one of the best materials for providing a support surface over your stud walls. It is relatively cheap and can be decorated in a number of ways. Essentially, the drywall is measured, cut, and fit against the stud walls, and then it is painted over. We have covered hanging the drywall in Chapter 13, so now we will move directly into the process of painting the drywall to make your house a true home.

Preparation

Begin by cleaning the room and covering the newly laid flooring. You will want to make sure that there are no obstructions in reaching floor or ceiling. Place drop cloths to prevent spillage or drips.

Place painter's tape around electrical switches or outlets, door frames, windows, or other areas which you wish to have free of paint. You can also assign a designated area for the mixing of paint and the storage of tools.

When purchasing your paint, the sales advisor will be able to offer advice. They will be able to advise you on the proper brush or roller for the job, as well as the finish offered by each. Also, the material of the roller will depend upon the nature of the paint. Water-based and latex paints will require synthetic brushes, while alkyd- and oil-based paints will require natural brushes.

Shake the paint well and mix it with a piece of wood prior to application. If you use several cans of paint, mix them together in a tub before painting to ensure that the color is uniform.

Remove all dust or dirt from the drywall before painting. If you are working in damp conditions, close all doors and windows and use a dehumidifier.

Work from the top down. If beginning with the ceiling, work from the ceiling to the tops of the walls, and then bring the roller down to the floor. If you choose not to paint the ceiling, then simply work from the tops of the walls down to the floor. Remember to cover the meeting of walls and ceiling with painter's tape.

When painting with a roller, use long strokes, working all the way from top to bottom. Place the next roller stripe at the halfway point of the previous. This will ensure that the thickness and color is consistent. You will also want to apply several layers of paint thinly, rather than attempting a few thick layers. This will offer a more consistent and aesthetic finish.

Remove the painter's tape once the paint has dried. A hairdryer can be used to loosen the bond of the tape before removal. Once the tape has been removed, trim the remaining space with small brushes, taking care not to paint past the desired limit.

Real Wood Walls
One alternative to placing drywall is the use of real wood. When covering your stud walls with real wood, you will want to first cover the insulation-filled stud walls with Visqueen. Stretch the Visqueen over the wall space and affix it to the studs with nails. Once the plastic sheet has been placed, you are ready to begin applying your real-wood finish to the stud walls.

There are countless options for real wood walls, but one which will demonstrate the principle is to use tongue-and-groove pine slats. Begin placing the slats against the studs, working from the floor to the ceiling. Stagger the joints, and fix the slats to the studs. In essence, this is a fairly simple application. You will need to measure the excess length of each board and cut it to length. The final row will need to be cut to width in the same manner.

This will offer a beautiful wall finish, with the feel of a log cabin. It is one of the simplest and yet most aesthetically pleasing finishes that you can provide your home, and though a bit time consuming, is fairly easy, even with limited tools and skills.

The image below shows pine walls in the process of installation:

Fitting pine walls

Finishing Interior Walls – Checklist

- Choose the finish for your interior walls. You may opt for painted drywall, paneling, drywall veneer, real wood, or the other options mentioned above.
- If choosing to use painted drywall, prepare the drywall to receive paint and prepare the area to protect it from spillage or excess paint by using drop cloths and painters tape. After the paint has dried, trim the edges of walls and around light switches and power outlets.
- If choosing to panel the walls with real wood, stagger the joints and line the edges up with the battens. Remember that drywall is unnecessary for this design option.

Chapter 16 – Exterior Finishes

Finishing the exterior of your container, like every step of the process, offers a number of options. One of the key considerations in this process is whether or not you have insulated the exterior of your container. Though you will be able to finish the exterior of the container with cladding even if you have placed foam insulation on the exterior, it will be far more challenging and will compromise your insulation. Therefore, here are some recommended methods for finishing the exterior of your home, depending upon the insulation of the exterior.

Finishing an Exterior with External Insulation

If you have placed spray foam insulation on the exterior of your home, then you have only a few recommended options. The first is to paint, and the next is to cover the insulation with stucco. Either way, you will want to ensure that your insulation is covered and sealed. When closed-cell polyurethane is exposed to sunlight, it begins to degrade. Paint or stucco will ensure that your insulation remains intact and retains its integrity.

Painting Exterior Insulation

When painting over exterior insulation, remember to use either latex paint or water-based acrylic. Oil-based paints can damage the foam of the insulation. Avoid high-gloss paints, as these will highlight any unevenness in the underlying surface. Flat or semi-gloss paints will help to both cover the insulation and provide an aesthetic finish.

Prior to painting, walk around the container and keep an eye out for rough edges. If you do see any rough edges, sand them down with sandpaper. Remember to wear a facemask in the process to avoid inhaling particles of insulation.

Once all rough edges have been removed, you can cover the exterior with paint. Use a minimum of three coats. It can be applied with either a spray gun, roller, or thick brush. Spray guns are the quickest option and offer the most consistent paint cover. Make sure to gauge the paint flow on scrap cardboard before beginning application. Rollers will be slightly slower, but will get the job done effectively. Paintbrushes offer the best control, but get the slowest results.

Tips: You may choose to apply wax sealant to cover the paint once it has been applied. You will get a better finish if you use several thin coats rather than a single or few thick coats. Each layer should be allowed to dry before applying a new one.

Rendering or Stuccoing the Exterior

If you choose to stucco the exterior of your home, it is best to first ensure that the spray foam insulation has been applied with a rough finish. This will ensure that the surface has more texture for the stucco to grip. Since the render is just for finish, there's no need to go overboard with it. You can simply purchase just-add-water mixes. Each 20kg bag will offer 5mm of cover to a 2.5m^2 (50 ft^2) of surface area.

The first step in applying stucco to your home is to fix beading to the corners with adhesive, ensuring that the beading is straight. Cover the ground around the exterior of your home with thick plastic sheets. Mix the stucco powder in a bucket with water, and allow to stand for five minutes. While waiting, wet the external insulation down with a hose, providing a damp surface for the stucco to affix to.

Begin applying the stucco from the bottom of the container and work upwards, using a steel trowel. Use long strokes to ensure that it is applied evenly across the surface. Make sure that all stucco is applied within 30 minutes after mixing. As with paint, it is better to place the stucco in multiple thin layers rather than a few thick ones. Try to keep each layer about 5mm. Rake each layer after application and while still wet. This will offer grip for the next layer. Finish the last layer with a polystyrene float, giving a nice finish to the stucco.

Finishing an Exterior without External Insulation

If you have chosen to leave the exterior of your container home bare of insulation, then you can finish it in a number of ways. One of the simplest, easiest, and cheapest is to leave it bare. This showcases the origin of your home, and can be quite aesthetically pleasing, as well as a tangible indication of what you have accomplished in the creation of your home.

If you choose not to leave it bare, then you can either paint the surface or clad it with wood. Leaving the containers plain offers no more explanation, so the following sections will explore the process of both painting and cladding with wood.

Painting your Container

While leaving your container bare can leave a legacy as to the origins of your container, it also leaves it susceptible to the elements. By adding a layer of paint, you protect against rust and increase the longevity of your homes.

The first step is to prepare your containers. Peel off any stickers and clean the surface of your containers. You can use a razor blade if the stickers are proving difficult to remove by hand. Should any rust remain, remove it with sandpaper, grinders, or wire brushes. You will also want to cover the ground surrounding your container with thick plastic sheets.

The best paint to apply to the exterior is alkyd enamel paint. This can be applied to the exterior either with brushes, rollers, or spray guns. As described above, spray guns are the fastest option and provide the most consistent cover. Rollers are slightly slower, but can still offer a fairly consistent cover. Paintbrushes offer the most control, but require the most skill to ensure a consistent application. Use a minimum of three coats when applying exterior paint.

Timber Cladding your Exterior

The final option that we will explore in this manual for finishing the exterior of your home is cladding it with timber. This offers an aesthetically pleasing option, giving your home the external appearance of a wood home. It is light and quick to fit, and it can also provide an additional layer of protection to the exterior of your home.

The first step in timber cladding your home is to fit the battens: 2 x 4 in. planks are ideal for this process, and it is best to fit them to the size of the container before framing your container. Fit the battens 400mm (16 in.) apart. Fix them to the container by drilling a hole through the end of each batten 1 ft. from both floor and roof. Drive a bolt through this hole and tighten a bolt on the inside of the container to hold the batten in place.

After the battens have been affixed at top and bottom, drill a hole each foot and repeat the process, tightening a screw on the inside of the container for each one. The battens will be attached to the container securely.

Once your battens are in place around the perimeter of the container, you will be able to attach cladding to them. Cladding is essentially wooden boards nailed onto the exterior battens. The process is essentially the same as adding real wood to the interior walls. Nail the cladding into the battens using stainless steel nails. Begin at the bottom of the battens and work your way up to the top. Overlap the joints of the cladding as shown in the figure below. Once the cladding has been placed, treat it with a moisture and UV resistant coating.

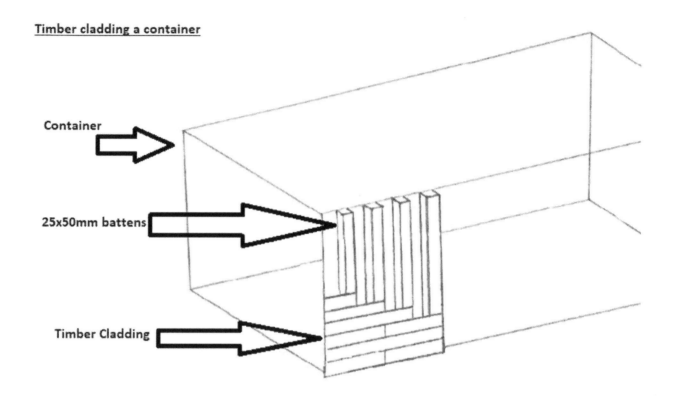

Timber cladding a container

Container →

25x50mm battens →

Timber Cladding →

Finishing Your Exterior – Checklist

- Select your desired exterior, keeping in mind the preferable options for insulated and uninsulated exteriors.
- If you choose to paint an exterior without insulation, make sure to remove all stickers and rust.
- If you choose to paint an insulated exterior, use latex or water-based acrylic paints.
- If you choose to paint an exterior without insulation, use alkyd enamel paints.
- Use a minimum of three coats. Remember that many thin layers of paint will produce a better finish than a few thick layers.
- For cladding your exterior with timber, begin by lining the exterior with battens. Drill holes through the top and bottom of each batten and the container behind it. Drive bolts through the holes and thread a nut on the bolt on the inside of the container.
- Line the battens with wood, going from the bottom up and alternating the edges on different battens.
- Seal the cladding with moisture and UV resistant sealant.

Chapter 17 – Final Words

We have now covered all the steps you need to address in creating your shipping container home. It should be apparent now how many choices you have.

Making a home is one of the most fulfilling DIY projects that any person can embark upon. It leaves you with a gift that will house the family for many years to come. To offer a bit more inspiration, we will leave you with a number of examples of completed shipping container homes, showing how amazing they can be once they are finished. Enjoy!

One Container Homes:

Photograph by Nicolás Boullosa - **https://www.flickr.com/photos/faircompanies/19815406413**

Photograph by Nicolás Boullosa - https://www.flickr.com/photos/faircompanies/20436353715

The containers above both show single container homes, offering exterior and interior view. You can see how much value can be packed within a tiny space, and how the exterior of the home can be decorated to make a home with the greatest aesthetic value.

Below are a few examples of more complex designs. While you can make your home as simple and economic as possible, you can also choose to construct a shipping container home on the basis of luxury. Below, you will see shipping container constructions made as apartments and as luxury homes. The options are limited only by your imagination and budget.

Container City II

Photograph by plentyofants - **https://www.flickr.com/photos/plentyofants/683994728**

Other container homes

Shipping container homes are the way of the future. They use readily available materials to make homes exactly to your specifications at a fraction of the cost of a traditional home. Green, sustainable housing, cheap materials, quick construction. You can have a home as simple and luxurious as you want, after putting in a minimum of time and energy.

Many people dream of building their own home, but often this dream seems out of reach. Hopefully, this manual has shown you that it *is* possible. More than that, it's relatively simple. Enjoy the process of building your home, and take a step into greater self-sufficiency!

Can you help me?

Did you enjoy this book? If so, can you please leave a review for the book on Amazon? Thank you very much for your support.

Made in the USA
Lexington, KY
26 March 2018